GW00730254

NICARAGUAN COOKING

NICARAGUAN COOKING

My Grandmother's Recipes

Trudy Espinoza-Abrams

Copyright © 2003 Trudy Espinoza-Abrams.

Library of Congress Number: 2003098608
ISBN: Softcover   1-4134-3779-6

All rights reserved. No part of this book may be reproduced, stored in
a retrieval system, or transmitted by any means, electronic, mechanical,
photocopying, recording, or otherwise, without written permission from
the author.

This book was printed in the United States of America.

To order additional copies of this book, contact:
Xlibris Corporation
1-888-795-4274
www.Xlibris.com
Orders@Xlibris.com
21479

CONTENTS

For my daughters, Jessina, Erin, Karen, and Deirdre.

In memory of my grandmother, and of my grandfather, who so much enjoyed eating her cooking

ACKNOWLEDGEMENTS

Thanks to:

My husband, for his taste buds, his patience, his proofreading, and his encouragement. I could not have written this book without him.

My daughters, for pressing on me the importance of writing down these recipes for their future use, so that they would not get lost for the generations to come.

My very dear aunt, Lydia Sandino, for discussing—and helping clarify—some of the recipes with me.

And to my cousin, Marlon Espinoza, for sharing many anecdotes of my grandparents.

PREFACE

I began writing down these recipes years ago, just so my daughters would have something from my country to refer to in the future. But one recipe inevitably led to another, as a taste or an aroma would open a floodgate of sensations, transporting me to a long-ago time, when, as a young girl, I stood in the kitchen at my grandmother's side, absorbing the sounds and smells, as she prepared the thousands of meals we enjoyed from her hand.

In later years, grown up and with a family of my own, I also, many times, asked my grandmother (who lived to the ripe old age of ninety-six) the forgotten details of many of her recipes. The recipes set down here are the ones she learned from her mother, and I, in turn, am sharing them with you.

The essence of my grandmother's approach to cooking was to use the freshest and most natural ingredients and prepare them using simple traditional methods. (For example, she always hand-ground her own corn for tortillas, using a primitive mortar and pestle, unchanged in any significant way for more than one thousand years, and still available today in Hispanic markets throughout the world.)

The recipes come not only from my hometown, Granada, but also from several other areas of the country that grandmother traveled through as a child, when she and her mother left their home to escape the civil strife within the country, often having to make do with what they were able to find in the countryside.

The glossary, at the end of this book, defines all of the uncommon Spanish-language words and food terms used below. Unless you are fluent in Spanish, you will probably need to consult it regularly, as you browse through the following recipes.

APPETIZERS

Vigorón (Yucca with Pork)

3 large fresh yuccas (about 3½-4 pounds)
5 cups of water
½ white head of cabbage, finely shredded
2 large tomatoes, finely chopped
juice of 1 lime
2 tablespoons of white vinegar
¼ cup of water
4-5 *congo* peppers, mashed
1 pound of *chicharron* (pork fried skin), cut up in bite size
salt and ground black pepper to taste

In Nicaragua, this dish is served on a banana leaf as a *merienda* (snack). It is very popular at the beach during the summer, or at the *kioskos* (food stands) in the Central Park, where it is served throughout the day and evening. Sometimes, it is eaten as an early dinner. It is often accompanied by *chicha* (a fermented corn drink).

Fresh yucca should be firm to the touch, with a light brown skin. Trim the ends of the yucca and cut into 2½-inch lengths. Make a lengthwise incision along each piece and pull the skin up from the meat with the end of the knife—it should come off easily. Do this to each piece.

Wash the yucca pieces in cool water and put them in a deep stockpot with 5 cups of water and a large pinch of salt for flavor.

Bring to a boil, then lower to medium heat, and continue boiling for another 5-7 minutes, until the yucca begins to burst open.

Meanwhile combine the cabbage, tomatoes, lime juice, vinegar, remaining water, and Chili Congo (how much chili to add depends on how spicy you like it). Mix well and check that it is not too acidic. Add salt and pepper.

To serve, place some yucca pieces on a plate, add some chicharron on top, followed by the cabbage salad; the finished Vigorón should have a layered look.

Serves 4-5.

Tortitas de Carne (Beef Patties)

1 pound of ground beef
2 carrots, peeled, finely chopped
1 potato, peeled, finely chopped
½ small red bell pepper, finely chopped
1 onion, finely chopped
3 garlic cloves, minced
1 cup of flour or 3 cups of bread crumbs
1 egg
3 tablespoons of vegetable oil
salt and ground black pepper to taste

This dish is also served as a main course. Put the ground beef in a large bowl. Add the potato, carrots, red bell pepper, onion, flour, egg, salt, black pepper, and garlic; mix well. With a teaspoon, take some of the mixture and form it into a ball; then, press the ball flat like a pancake. In a medium frying pan, add enough vegetable oil to fry the meat patty until brown on both sides. Serve it with Salsa de Chile.

Makes approximately 15 servings.

Repocheta (Fried Stuffed Tortilla)

½ pound of *queso fresco* or 1 package (8 ounces) of cream cheese
2 handmade tortillas or 6 Mexican tortillas
1 medium onion, finely chopped
½ cup of white vinegar
1 cup of water
½ cup of vegetable oil
1 teaspoon of serrano pepper, finely chopped
salt and ground black pepper to taste

Cut the homemade tortillas in quarters, open and spread out one edge of each quarter and fill with cheese. Heat the oil in a frying pan and put the Repocheta in. Cook on both sides until the top of the tortilla is slightly golden. If using Mexican tortillas, spread the cheese over each one, roll it into a tube, and fry it.

Mix the onion with the vinegar, water, serrano pepper, salt, and black pepper to taste. Pour over the Repochetas when serving.

Serves about 12.

Ceviche de Pescado (Fish Ceviche)

1 pound of fresh whitefish
½ cup of onion
juice of 5 limes
½ teaspoon of oregano leave
1 teaspoon of chopped serrano pepper
10 cilantro stems, finely chopped
salt and ground black pepper to taste
¼ cup of red bell pepper, chopped

All of the ingredients should be finely chopped. Mix them all together and squeeze the juice of the limes to cover the whole mixture. Use more lime juice if needed. Let the mixture sit in the refrigerator, covered, for 2-3 days until the acid of the lemon "cooks" the fish, turning it pure white and soft enough to chew easily. We also follow this recipe when making Shrimp Ceviche or Conch Ceviche.

Decorate with parsley and serve with salted crackers on the side.

Serves 4.

Guacamol (Guacamole)

2 ripe Hass avocados (These are the dark-skinned kind.)
2 large eggs, hard boiled
¼ cup of onion
¼ cup of red bell pepper
1 garlic clove, minced
juice of 3 limes
1 large ripe tomato, seeded
1 teaspoon of serrano pepper
6 cilantro sprigs
salt and ground black pepper to taste
pinch of sugar

Chop all the ingredients in small pieces. In a medium bowl, mix everything until well coated with the lime juice. Add more salt if needed. Serve with tortilla chips.

This is the way Guacamole is served in my country. However, some people prefer it as a smooth dip, in which case, you can mash the ingredients. Do not use metal utensils or containers as this turns the avocado brown.

Serves 6.

Papas Rellenas (Stuffed Potatoes)

1 cup of ground beef stew
1 teaspoon of *achiote* paste
2 limes
6 medium potatoes
1 egg
¼ cup of olive oil
2 cups of water
4 cilantro sprigs, finely chopped
salt and ground black pepper to taste
1 garlic clove, minced

Wash and rinse the potatoes. In saucepan, bring them to a boil in 2 cups of water until tender. Remove from heat and let cool. Remove the skin.

In large bowl, mash the potatoes until smooth but not pasty. Dilute the achiote paste in the lime juice and add it to the potatoes together with the salt, black pepper, garlic, and cilantro. Mix well. Take a heaping tablespoon of dough and flatten it. In the center of each piece, place some of the meat mixture. Fold the dough over; pinch the ends, so the mixture doesn't come out.

In a large bowl, beat the egg white until fluffy, and then slowly add the yolk, beating continuously. Fold the potato in the egg mixture. In a large skillet, heat the oil and fry each potato until golden brown; then, turn over and fry the other side. Remove and garnish with pickled onions.

Serves 8.

Ceviche de Plátano Verde (Plantain Ceviche)

1 green plantain
1 small onion
1 medium tomato, seeded
5 key limes, juice squeezed out
1 teaspoon of serrano pepper, seeded
½ teaspoon of Worcestershire sauce
½ cup of cilantro
salt and ground black pepper to taste
5 parsley sprigs, for garnish

Three days before serving: Remove the skin from the plantain and cut lengthwise, removing the inside woody vein. Chop the plantain, tomato, serrano pepper, onion, and cilantro in very small pieces. Mix all of the ingredients together, except for the parsley, in a glass or ceramic bowl; refrigerate, stirring the mixture from time to time.

Serves 4-6.

Queso Frito (Fried Cheese)

½ pound of queso del Caribe or queso fresco
4 tablespoons of vegetable oil

In a skillet, warm up the oil over medium heat. Cut the cheese in ½-inch slices. Fry both sides until golden brown. Remove. Place over paper towel to drain. Cut in squares and serve over Tostones, over a tortilla with tomato salsa, or as a side dish to Gallo Pinto.

Makes 6-8 pieces.

Anticuchos (Beef Heart)

2 large beef hearts (about 2 pounds each)
3 garlic cloves, minced

4 green onions (scallions), cut small
juice of 4 limes
½ cup of water
1 teaspoon of *achiote* paste
½ teaspoon of serrano pepper
salt and ground black pepper to taste
2 tablespoons of vegetable oil for frying

This dish is also served as a main course.

The day before, very carefully clean the hearts of any fat, valves, ligaments, and membranes still attached. Cut lengthwise into strips, and put in a large bowl. Dissolve the achiote paste in the lime juices and add it to the bowl, together with the rest of the ingredients. Marinate overnight in the refrigerator, turning the pieces every now and then to gather the flavors.

When ready to cook, place the oil in a skillet over medium-high heat, and fry the pieces for a minute on each side—less if you like it very rare, which is the way it should be served. Remove and set aside in a serving dish. Fry the onions and the marinade until reduced and thickened. Put over the heart and serve.

Serves about 4-5.

Yoltamale (Sweet Tamale)

30 ears of corn
1½ pounds of *crema fresca* (found in most Mexican grocery stores)
2 pounds of *añejo* cheese
2 tablespoons of salt
2 cups of sugar
2 cups of milk
1 cup of water
pinch of salt

Remove the husks from the ears of corn, being careful not to break them. Wash and dry them well; put aside to use later. Scrape the kernels from the ears with a sharp knife and finely mash the corn together with the cheese. While mashing, slowly add the salt, sugar, and milk; mix well.

Take 2 cornhusks and place the 2 largest ends together, one on top of the other. Over each leaf, put ¾ tablespoon of the mixture, close the husk, and fold the ends toward the center to complete the tamale. Continue doing the same thing with the rest of the mixture and remaining husks, saving a few to line the pot.

Arrange these husks from bottom to top of a deep large pot. Arrange the tamales one on top of another, until the pot is full. Add the cup of water and steam the tamales over low heat for 2 hours. Let them cool for at least 30 minutes before serving so they firm up.

Makes about 15 servings. Can be served sliced with a cube of cheese on top or used as a side dish.

Variation:

15-20 cans (15¼-ounces) of corn (reserve the water to steam the tamales in)
30 dried large cornhusks (found at the Mexican markets)
3 cups of water

Put the cornhusks in a large pot with the water and boil for about 10 minutes. Remove and drain. Follow directions as above.

Tamale

2 cups of *masa harina*
½ cup of water
2½ tablespoons of vegetable shortening

1 large garlic glove, minced
1½ teaspoons of onion, finely chopped
½ teaspoon of oregano powder
1 teaspoon of *achiote* paste
2 tablespoons of vinegar
1 medium potato, cooked and mashed
5 cilantro sprigs
5 mint sprigs
salt and ground black pepper to taste
10 large cornhusk leaves for wrapping

Place all of the above ingredients, beginning with the water, in a food processor. Mix thoroughly until well blended and doughy.

Take each leaf, open it, and place a golf-ball-sized piece of dough in the middle; flatten the dough and wrap the husk around it; then, fold over the end without any dough. Continue the same procedure with the other leaves.

In a bamboo or metal steamer with 1½ cup of water in the bottom, place all of the tamales in the top section and steam for 60 minutes, until the dough is springy to the touch.

For slight variations, I have filled the tamales by adding 2 teaspoons of refried black or red beans, cooked shredded pork, or cooked shredded chicken to the top of the dough before folding it over and wrapping it.

Makes 10 tamales.

Side Dishes

Pan de Revueltas (Corn and Cheese Bread)

½ cup of all-purpose white flour
½ teaspoon of sugar
¼ cup of yellow cornmeal
¾ cup of water, or more if needed
½ cup of masa harina
1 large egg, lightly beaten
½ teaspoon of baking powder
$^{1}/_{3}$ cup of *sincho* cheese
1 tablespoon of vegetable oil
½ teaspoon of salt
1 can (8-ounce) of creamy sweet corn (optional)

Heat oven to 375°F. Mix everything together. Bake in a greased pan (9 x 12 x 2 inches) for about 45 minutes. It is done when an inserted knife comes out clean.

Serves 6.

Plátanos Cocidos (Boiled Plantains)

2 green or yellow plantains
1 cup of water
salt to taste
¼ pound of queso fresco, cut in bite sizes

If cooking green plantains, remove the skin and discard. Cut the plantains in halves. Place in a medium pan with the water and salt. When the water starts to boil, lower the heat and cook for about 15-18 minutes. Cut in bite sizes and place raw or fried cheese over them. Serve as accompaniment to meals or as tapas.

If cooking ripe yellow plantains, cut only the ends, leaving the rest of the skin on while cooking. These are cooked for less time, 10-12 minutes. When done, put under cold water. Remove the skin and scrape all around the plantain with the dull side of a knife, to remove any leftover, stringy material.

Serves 6.

Tostones (Refried Plantain Patties)

½ cup of vegetable oil, for frying
2 green plantains, peeled, cut into 1-inch-thick rounds
salt for sprinkling

In a frying pan, heat the oil over moderate heat. Carefully, add 6-7 plantain rounds; fry until lightly yellow on both sides. Remove. Place on paper towels to drain. Repeat with the rest.

Place a plantain round between 2 pieces of paper towel and mash flat with your hand. Do the same with the remaining plantains.

Return plantain rounds to oil; refry until golden brown. Transfer to paper towels; sprinkle with salt.

Tostones can be served with cheese on top (cream cheese, queso fresco, queso sincho, or fried cheese), with Mojo con Ajo, or simply as an accompaniment to other dishes instead of bread or tortillas

Serves 12.

Revueltas (Tortillas with Cheese)

1 cup of masa harina
½ cup of *sincho* cheese, finely ground
²/₃ cup of water
2 tablespoons of vegetable oil
¼ teaspoon of salt
metal spatula

My *abuelita* (grandmother) would make Revueltas early in the morning, so we could have them for breakfast. They were delicious, with a cup of sweetened black coffee, and the aroma of both permeated the air.

In a large bowl, combine the masa harina, cheese, and salt; mix together, adding the water a bit at a time until the dough is thoroughly mixed. This should have the consistency of pizza or baking dough, smooth and moist. More water may be required.

Place a piece of wax paper on a flat surface and put a portion of the dough, the size of a billiard ball or slightly smaller, on the middle of the paper and begin to flatten it in the shape of a pancake. The dough should be about ¼-inch thick and 7-inch diameter when flattened. Take the paper with the flattened dough, and invert the Revuelta over the palm of your other hand; then, remove the paper carefully. Do this with each one.

Meanwhile, place a flat skillet or comal over a burner on medium heat. Grease the skillet with oil and a paper towel. When the skillet is hot, place the Revuelta on it. Carefully, moisten the top side with water, so it won't dry out. Even though you have oiled the comal, the Revuelta will still get stuck to it because of the cheese. With the spatula, carefully pry the Revuelta from the skillet and flip it over to cook the other side. Both sides should be golden brown.

To make sure that the Revuelta is cooking inside, firmly and continuously pat it all over, while it is cooking, using a folded paper towel. The top layer should rise up a bit. Remove and wrap in a large cloth napkin to keep warm; serve immediately.

Makes about 3-4 Revueltas.

Tortillas de Maiz (Corn Tortillas)

1½ cups of masa harina
1 cup of water
3 tablespoons of vegetable oil
¼ teaspoon of salt
metal spatula

In a large bowl, mix the masa harina, 1 tablespoon of the vegetable oil, and the salt. Mix well. Add the water, a bit at a time, while kneading the dough, until it has the consistency of pizza or baking dough, smooth and moist. Add more water, if too dry.

Place a piece of wax paper on a flat surface and put a portion of the dough, the size of a billiard ball or slightly smaller, on the middle of the paper and begin to flatten it in the shape of a pancake. The dough should be about ¼-inch thick and 7-inch diameter when flattened. Take the paper with the flattened dough, and invert the tortilla over the palm of your other hand; then, remove the paper carefully. Do this to each one.

Meanwhile, place a flat skillet or comal over a burner on medium heat. Grease the skillet with oil and a paper towel. When the skillet is hot, place the tortilla on it. Carefully, moisten the top side with water, so it won't dry out. Even though you have oiled the comal, sometimes the tortilla will still get stuck to it. With the spatula, carefully pry the tortilla from the skillet and flip it over to cook the other side. Both sides should be golden brown.

To make sure that the tortilla is cooking inside, firmly and continuously pat it all over, while it is cooking, using a folded paper towel. The top layer should rise up, creating a pocket. Remove the tortilla and wrap it in a large cloth napkin to keep warm; serve immediately.

Don't throw away old tortillas; they are used for making other dishes that you will find throughout this book.

Makes about 3-4 tortillas of about 7-inch diameter.

Pan de Maiz (Corn Bread)

2½ cups of white flour
$^1/_3$ cup of cornmeal
½ teaspoon of salt
2 tablespoons of sugar
2 tablespoons of vegetable oil
$^2/_3$ cup of milk
2 tablespoons of water
1 large egg
1 small can (8-ounces) of creamy sweet corn

Combine all the ingredients except the corn in a large mixing bowl. Mix well, and then add the corn. Grease the bottom and sides of a large iron skillet, and pour in the mixture. Cook covered on the burner under low-medium heat for about 20-30 minutes, or until an inserted toothpick comes out clean. You can also bake it at 350°F, until golden brown, about 30 minutes

Serves 8.

Tortas de Maiz (Cornmeal Pancakes)

¾ cup of all-purpose flour
¾ cup of yellow cornmeal
2 teaspoons of baking powder
½ teaspoon of salt
1 teaspoon of sugar
1 large egg, lightly beaten
1½ cups of low-fat milk
2 tablespoons of vegetable oil
1 small can (8-ounces) of creamy sweet corn

Mix all of the ingredients together. In a large well-oiled skillet placed over medium heat, spread ¼ cup of batter onto the surface. Cook until the top begins to bubble and the bottom is golden. Flip over and cook until golden. Repeat with remaining batter. Stack the pancakes on a serving plate. When serving, top each individual pancake with a dollop of sour cream (I personally use yogurt instead), then some cooked red or black beans, and finish off with tomato salsa on top.

Serves 4.

Arroz Frito (Fried White Rice)

1 cup of white rice
½ small onion, chopped
2 tablespoons of vegetable oil
2 cups of hot water
½ teaspoon of salt
2 tablespoons of green or red bell peppers, chopped finely

In a frying pan placed over medium heat, fry the bell pepper until soft, followed by the onions. When the onions are translucent, add the rice and fry to a light golden color. Slowly, pour in the water; add the salt. Stir gently only once, and then bring to a medium boil. When the surface of the rice is dry but you can still hear some bubbling, cover and turn the heat to low; then, cook for another 10-15 minutes.

Check the rice for doneness by taking just a few of the grains from the top, without disturbing the rest. If still a bit chewy, sprinkle some water over the top, cover again, and continue cooking for another 5 minutes. If the texture is good and the rice is tender, slowly bring the bottom rice to the top using a fork and stir gently; then, serve. Overall cooking time is approximately 45-50 minutes.

Serves 4-5.

BREAKFAST

Huevos Revueltos (Scrambled Eggs)

4 eggs
2 tablespoons of vegetable oil
salt and ground black pepper to taste
3 tablespoons of finely chopped onion
¼ cup of chopped cilantro

In a small bowl, whisk the eggs, salt, and pepper until thoroughly blended. Heat the oil in a skillet and fry the onion until translucent. Add the eggs, and stir while cooking. Remove when done as desired and place on serving dish. Sprinkle with the chopped cilantro.

Salsa Sofrita instead of cilantro, is sometimes added on top of the scrambled eggs after placing them on the serving dish. (We also use Salsa Sofrita on top of whole fried eggs just before serving them.)

Serves 3.

Huevos Rancheros (Rancheros Eggs)

4 eggs
2 tablespoons of vegetable oil
salt and ground black pepper to taste
2 tablespoons of finely chopped onion
2 tablespoons of green bell pepper, finely chopped
1 medium tomato, seeded, chopped
½ teaspoon of serrano pepper, seeded, chopped finely

In a small bowl, whisk the eggs, salt, and pepper until thoroughly blended. Heat the oil in a skillet over medium heat. Fry the green pepper first, followed by the onion and tomato. When the tomato is soft, add the eggs and continue frying, until these are lightly moist; stir while cooking.

Serves 3.

Huevos Revueltos con Chorizos
(Scrambled Eggs with Sausages)

6 eggs
1 large chorizo, 10-12 ounces (Chorizos have different levels of
    spiciness: mild, hot, and fire.)
salt and ground black pepper to taste

In a medium skillet, fry the sausage, until the oil has rendered out, while stirring and breaking the meat apart. This takes about 2 minutes.

In a small bowl, beat the eggs, salt, and pepper until well mixed. Pour the eggs in the chorizo. Stir while cooking. When the eggs are cooked but moist, remove and serve hot.

Serves 5-6.

Chorizos con Frijoles (Sausages Mixed with Bean)

3 small chorizos, 2.4 ounces
3 tablespoons of chopped onion
1½ cups of home-cooked beans or one 14-ounce can of red beans
1 tablespoon of vegetable oil
salt to taste

In a medium-sized skillet, fry the onion in the oil over medium heat until translucent. Add the chorizo and break it in small pieces, as you are frying it, for about 2 minutes. Add the beans and continue frying for 2-3 more minutes.

Chorizos are also delicious when fried with diced, boiled potatoes.

Serves 5-6.

Chorizos con Arroz (Sausages with Rice)

2 cups of cooked white rice
2 chorizos, 2.4 ounces
¼ cup of onion, chopped
½ cup of green bell pepper
salt and ground black pepper to taste

Fry the chorizos, while breaking them up, for about 2 minutes. Add the green pepper first, followed by the onion. When these are soft, add the cooked rice and continue stirring while frying, so that everything is well mixed, and the rice is coated with the oil from the sausage. When the chorizo is dry and crumbly, the dish is done.

Serves 4.

Torta de Huevo (Egg Torte with Rice)

¼ cup of cooked white rice
2 egg whites
¼ cup of chopped onion
¼ cup of chopped red bell pepper
salt and ground black pepper to taste
1 teaspoon of serrano pepper, chopped
2 tablespoons of vegetable oil
¼ cup of chopped cilantro

In a frying pan, heat the oil and fry the red pepper, onion, and serrano pepper. Remove from pan and set aside.

In a small bowl, whisk the egg whites until fluffy. Add the rice, condiments, salt, and pepper, folding everything in except the cilantro. Add the mixture to the frying pan and fry first one side and then the other over medium heat until golden. Remove from pan and sprinkle with chopped cilantro before serving.

Serves 2.

Chorizos de Casa (Homemade Sausages)

1 pound of ground pork
4 garlic cloves, minced
½ teaspoon of *achiote* paste
½ cup of sliced onion
½ teaspoon of salt, or to taste
¼ teaspoon of freshly ground black pepper
1 tablespoon of vinegar, diluted with ¼ cup of water
1 teaspoon of finely chopped serrano pepper

Dissolve the achiote in the vinegar-water solution. Combine the pork, garlic, onion, salt, and pepper to make a coarse mixture. Add the achiote solution and mix well.

Fry the mixture in a skillet over moderate heat for 10 to 12 minutes, until it is lightly browned and thoroughly cooked. The chorizo should be moist, with a bit of sauce remaining in the pan. You can make the mixture the day before cooking it and keep it refrigerated.

Serve hot with tortillas or use it with eggs.

Serves 6.

Frijoles Fritos (Fried Beans)

2 cups of red beans
$^1/_8$ cup onion, chopped fine
2 tablespoons of vegetable oil
salt and ground black pepper to taste

In a skillet over moderate heat, fry the chopped onion in the vegetable oil and when soft and translucent, add the beans and salt if needed. Fry the beans until dried and beginning to look toasted.

Serves 2-3.

Nacatamal (Corn and Pork Tamale)

Masa

2 cups of masa harina
½ cup of water
4 tablespoons of vegetable shortening or lard
1 teaspoon of garlic, minced
1½ teaspoons of onion, finely chopped
½ teaspoon of oregano
1 teaspoon of annatto paste
2 tablespoons of vinegar
½ teaspoon of salt to taste
2 tablespoons of milk
1 cup of cooked mashed potatoes (2 medium potatoes)
5 fresh mint leaves, finely chopped
Aluminum foil cut into 15-inch squares for wrapping

Mix everything together and knead well.

Filling

1½ pounds of boneless pork, cut up into 2-inch cubes (You may substitute chicken or turkey.)
½ pound of *tocino* (salt pork), sliced in pieces
¼ cup of sour orange juice (juice of 1 lime and 1 grapefruit)
1 teaspoon of salt
1 teaspoon of serrano pepper, finely chopped
2 teaspoons of *achiote* paste
1 garlic clove, crushed
1 medium onion, sliced
1 tablespoon of sugar
½ cup of red bell pepper, chopped
½ cup of water

Mix all of the ingredients together. Set aside for about 1 hour for the meat to absorb the flavors of the marinade. Save the liquid for steaming.

Garnishes (2 slices of each vegetable, plus 1 teaspoon of rice, and ¼ teaspoon of serrano pepper for each tamale)

2 large potatoes, sliced ¼-inch thick
2 large tomatoes, sliced
2 medium onions, sliced
2 red bell peppers, sliced
20 fresh mint sprigs
½ cup of rice, well rinsed
20 stuffed green olives
2 serrano peppers, finely chopped
20 raisins (optional)
1 package banana leaves for wrapping

Cross 2 banana leaves at their centers and spread about 3 heaping tablespoons of the prepared Masa mixture in the middle. Add the ingredients in the following order: rice, 2 pork cubes, potatoes, tomatoes, onions, green olives, 2 mint sprigs, ¼ teaspoon of serrano pepper, and 2 slices of salt pork. Bring together the opposite ends of the leaves, fold them, and turn the Nacatamal over. Do the same with the other 2 ends, overlapping them. For added security so that no water will seep into the dough during cooking, wrap the Nacatamal in tinfoil and tie with a string. Do the same with the rest.

In a very deep large pot, place some banana leaves vertically from the bottom up to the top. Place the Nacatamales one on top of the other. Pour the juice remaining from the marinade with all the condiments into the pot, adding 1 cup of water. Bring to a boil, then turn heat down to medium-low, and cook for 4-6 hours. If boiling too hard, turn flame to low. Keep hot water on the side to add to the pot, as the water is consumed.

Nacatamales are eaten on Sundays for breakfast or lunch, rarely for dinner. They are accompanied by bread and sometimes Gallo Pinto on the side.

Makes about 12-15 servings.

Gallo Pinto (Red Beans and Rice)

This is my way of making Gallo Pinto (painted rooster, because of the red-and-white coloring). However, in Nicaragua, it is usually made with leftover beans and rice, fried together in vegetable oil and sliced onions.

1 pound of dried red beans
4 cups of long-grained rice
1 medium onion, finely chopped
1 garlic clove, minced
¼ cup of green pepper, finely chopped
8 cups of water for cooking
6 tablespoons of olive oil
1 bay leaf

1 teaspoon of dried basil leaf
1 teaspoon of oregano
salt and ground black pepper to taste
1 piece (about 1½-inch length by 1-inch diameter) of ginger root,
    peeled and cut lengthwise
5 bacon slices, finely chopped, optional
Extra water for soaking

Wash, rinse, and soak the beans for about 2 hours, in enough warm water to cover them; discard the water.

In a large pot, put 2 tablespoons of olive oil and fry the garlic, pepper, and half of the onion until translucent. If using bacon, now is the time to fry it. When the bacon is cooked softly, add the beans and mix. Add the water, bay leaf, basil leaves, oregano, and ginger; bring to a boil. Cook covered over medium heat, until the beans are al dente.

In a large skillet, use and fry the onion in the remaining oil for a few seconds. Add the rice and continue frying, stirring constantly, until the rice is golden color; put the fried rice in the kettle with the beans; add the salt. Bring to a boil uncovered, until the water has evaporated. Lower to medium heat, if it's boiling too hard. When the water has evaporated, cover, turn the heat to low, and continue cooking for about 15 minutes.

Uncover and gently stir by bringing the rice from the bottom to the top. If, at this time, the rice is still a little al dente, sprinkle some water over the top of the rice, cover, and continue cooking for another 10 minutes.

Gallo Pinto is generally served for dinner and breakfast, if there is any leftover from the night before. Rarely it is served for lunch.

Serves 10.

Sauces and Accompaniments

One or more of the following dishes is included with almost every meal as a matter of course—a meal would not be considered complete without them.

Mojo Simple (Plain Mojo)

1 teaspoon of serrano pepper, chopped
3 tablespoons of finely chopped red bell pepper
1 tablespoon of finely chopped onion
3 tablespoons of lime juice
¾ cup of olive oil
salt to taste

Mix all of the above ingredients, and serve at room temperature as an accompaniment to Tostones, yucca *frita*, and other side dishes.

Mojo con Ajo (Mojo with Garlic)

Follow the recipe above but add 3 large garlic cloves, minced. Stir well and leave outside to gather flavor. Use as above.

The above 2 sauces are primarily Cuban but are used all over Latin America.

Salsa Criolla (Creole Sauce)

4 large tomatoes, sliced in circles
2 medium onions, sliced in circles
2 lemons
1 small jalapeño pepper, chopped small
salt and ground black pepper to taste
3 tablespoons of olive oil

In large frying pan and with the oil hot, fry the onions. When onions are translucent, add the tomatoes, jalapeño, and lemon juice. Add salt and pepper to taste. Serve over scrambled or fried eggs, fried fish, or almost any dish.

Serves 6.

Salsa de Tomate (Fresh Tomato Salsa)

6 tomatoes, seeded, chopped
½ cup of chopped red onion
½ cup of chopped cilantro
2 tablespoons of jalapeño, finely chopped
2 tablespoons of lime juice
2 tablespoons of vinegar
¼ cup of water
salt and ground black pepper to taste

In a serving bowl, mix all of the ingredients. Let it sit for 30 minutes at room temperature for flavors to blend. Serve with tortilla chips and over many other dishes. Can be kept refrigerated, tightly covered, for up to a week.

Makes about 2 cups.

Salsa Sofrita (Lightly Fried Salsa)

1 large red bell pepper, sliced
1 large onion, sliced
3 tomatoes, diced
juice of 1 lime
2 tablespoons of vegetable oil
1 teaspoon of jalapeño, chopped
salt and ground black pepper to taste

Heat the oil in a skillet and fry the red pepper first, then the onion, until translucent. Add the tomatoes, jalapeño, lime juice, salt, and pepper, cooking everything until soft. Serve over eggs, turtle, fried fish, etc.

Serves 8.

Salsa de Chile (Chili Sauce)

juice of 1 lime
½ cup of water
1 tablespoon of vinegar
5 Chili Congos, mashed, or 1 serrano pepper, chopped fine
salt and ground black pepper to taste

Mix everything together, use as desired (makes even plain rice taste delicious).

Encurtido de Repollo (Pickled Slaw)

½ head of white cabbage
4 medium onions, quartered
1 medium carrot, diced

1 tablespoon of serrano pepper, finely chopped
½ cup of white vinegar
¼ cup of apple cider vinegar
¼ cup of water
1½ teaspoons of oregano leaves
salt and black pepper to taste
2 cups of water, enough to cover cabbage

Immerse the cabbage in 2 cups of boiling water for a few seconds. Cut finely, lengthwise, into 1-inch strips. Add the rest of the ingredients, mixing everything together. Set aside to continue marinating in the vinegar for about 2 weeks. Serve as a side dish to almost any meal.

Cebollas Encurtidas (Pickled Onions)

8 medium onions, quartered
10 congo peppers, mashed, or 1 large jalapeño pepper, chopped
1 cup of apple cider vinegar
½ cup of white vinegar
¼ cup of water
salt and ground black pepper to taste
pinch of sugar

Mix everything together. Cover and leave at room temperature for at least 4-5 days before using. Can be kept refrigerated in a glass jar for up to a month. Make sure ingredients are covered with liquid. Serve as a side dish.

Cebollas Dulces (Sweet Onions)

2 large white sweet onions, sliced
juice of 2 limes
½ teaspoon of sugar
3 tablespoons of water
salt and ground black pepper to taste
chopped serrano pepper to taste

Mix all of the ingredients together. Let sit for a few hours, while the flavors develop and blend. Serve as accompaniment to Fufu, Stuffed Potatoes, and Taro Root Purée.

Soups

Sopa de Carne (Beef Soup)

This soup is also called Caldo de Res. My family likes it best with oxtail, which requires 2 oxtails of about 2-3 pounds each, and which usually come already cut into suitably sized pieces.

2 pounds of chuck beef, cut in 1½-inch cubes
3 pounds of soup marrow bones
1 pound of yucca, peeled, cut in 1½-inch lengths
2 large carrots, peeled, cut up
3 *malangas* (taro roots), peeled, quartered
2 chayotes, seeded, peeled, quartered
2 green Mexican squash, sliced
2 ears of corn, quartered
½ head of white cabbage, sliced
1 medium onion, sliced
2 garlic cloves, crushed
¼ cup of green bell pepper, sliced
2 large tomatoes, quartered
juice of 1 lime
½ teaspoon of cumin
6 *culantro* sprigs (usually found in Mexican markets)
salt and ground black pepper to taste
5-6 cups of water
1 teaspoon of jalapeño, optional
2 teaspoons of dried basil leaves or 4 fresh ones, cut

In a very large stockpot, place the meat, marrow bones, and water. Bring to a hard boil, removing the foam that forms on top. Do this for about 10 minutes. Add the onions, green pepper, garlic, jalapeño pepper, mint, basil, cumin, tomatoes, and lime juice. Continue boiling over medium to low heat, covered, for about 1½ hours, until the meat is tender. Add more water if needed.

Meanwhile, peel and cut the vegetables. When the meat is tender, add the vegetables one at a time, cooking them for about 3-4 minutes each before adding the next one, in the following order: yucca, chayote, malanga, cabbage slices, corn, squash (these 2 could go in together). It should take about 20-25 minutes to cook all of the vegetables on low to medium heat. Add salt and black pepper to taste. Cover the soup; turn the burner off and leave sitting for about half an hour to gather flavor before serving.

You can substitute other vegetables: pumpkin, plantains, sweet potatoes.

Serves 6-8.

Sopa de Arroz con Carne (Beef and Rice Soup)

1½ pounds of beef chuck, cubed
2 pounds of soup marrow bones
8 cups of water
1 large tomato, sliced
¼ cup of thin-sliced onions
2 garlic cloves, sliced thin
½ small red bell pepper, chopped
1 cup of raw rice
3 large carrots, peeled, cut
4 *culantro* sprigs (or mint, if culantro is unavailable)
¼ cup of sour orange

salt and ground black pepper to taste
½ teaspoon of serrano pepper (optional)

Place the meat, soup bones, and water in a very large pot. Bring to a hard boil, removing the foam that forms on top. Do this for about 10 minutes. Add all the other ingredients except the rice and carrots. Continue cooking over medium to low heat for 1 hour. Add the rice and carrots to the broth and continue simmering for another 30-40 minutes, until the rice and carrots are tender, but the rice is not mushy. Adjust salt if necessary.

This is a very simple, typical family recipe.

Serves 6.

Sopa de Queso (Cheese Soup)

1 cup of masa harina
1 teaspoon of annatto paste
1½ cups of *sincho* cheese, ground
1 small onion, sliced
2 eggs
2 tomatoes, sliced
4 mint sprigs
juice of 1 lime
¼ cup of vegetable oil
4 cans of chicken stock
2 cups of water
salt and ground black pepper to taste

Finely grind the cheese and mix it in a medium bowl with the masa harina and 1 tablespoon of the vegetable oil. In a small bowl, beat the eggs and pour them in the masa, mixing thoroughly. If the dough is too dry, add a couple of tablespoons of water and continue mixing. Take a tablespoon of the mixture and flatten it into a small, thick dumpling. In an oiled, heated skillet and over moderate heat, fry the dumplings until golden brown. The dough makes about 14-16 dumplings.

Meanwhile, in a large saucepan, boil the water and chicken stock with the onion, tomatoes, salt, and pepper. Dissolve the annatto paste in a little bit of water and a teaspoon of masa; add it to the pot. When the water is boiling, add the fried dumplings, mint, and lime juice, and simmer over low heat for another 10 minutes.

Serves 5-6.

Sopa de Mondongo/Menudo (Tripe Soup)

4 pounds of honeycomb tripe
3 pounds of pork feet, cut up
2 garlic cloves, crushed
juice of 4 limes
2 fresh ears of corn, quartered
¾ cup of rice
1 teaspoon of *achiote* paste
½ head of white cabbage, sliced
2 medium onions, sliced
4 medium tomatoes, sliced
2 large yuccas, peeled, cut up
salt and ground black pepper to taste
4 *culantro* leaves (You can substitute mint.)
1 small green bell pepper, chopped
2 tablespoons of baking soda
½ teaspoon of jalapeño, finely chopped
½ teaspoon of dried oregano
1 teaspoon of dried basil
½ teaspoon of dried cumin
5-6 cups of water
2 cups of sour orange (½ cup of sour orange juice = 2 lime juices
and 2 grapefruit juice; I often use the juice of 2 grapefruits to
wash the tripe rather than the sour orange mix.)

Clean the tripe of any excess fat; rinse in cold water. In a large bowl, wash the tripe thoroughly with the mixture of baking soda, sour orange, and the juice of 3 limes. After washing, let the tripe soak in fresh cold water with the skins of the citrus, for about 1 hour. Rinse. Cut the tripe in bite sizes; put in a large saucepan with 5 cups of water, ½ of the green pepper, 1 sliced onion, and 1 garlic clove. Cook for 3 hours until soft. Be sure there is always plenty of water covering the ingredients.

Meanwhile, in a small bowl, soak the rice for 30 minutes in 1 cup of water. Grind the rice in a blender or food processor with the rest of the green pepper, onion, garlic clove, 1 teaspoon of annatto paste, and the jalapeño. Add this mixture to the tripe with the rest of the condiments, the juice of 1 lime, culantro, and yucca. Continue cooking for another 20 minutes. Add the cabbage and cook for another 10 minutes; then, add the corn pieces and cook for 5 more minutes. Make sure that it has sufficient salt, lime, and chili to suit your taste. Turn the heat off and let it sit for about 30 minutes to gather flavor.

Serves 6-8.

Sopa de Frijoles Rojos (Red Beans Soup)

Home-cooked red beans:

1 pound of dried red beans
1 small onion, finely chopped
1 garlic clove, minced
¼ cup of red bell pepper, finely diced
½ teaspoon of ground cumin
1 teaspoon of dried oregano
ginger, peeled, about 1½-inch long
salt and ground black pepper to taste
8 cups of water
4-6 eggs, set aside

1 tablespoon of vegetable oil
sour cream, a dollop on top of each serving
1 pound of *chicharron* (fried pork rind)

(If omitting the chicharron, substitute two 14½-ounce cans of chicken stock for 4 of the 8 cups of water to add flavor to the soup.)

Soak the beans for about 2 hours in enough warm water to cover, or parboil them for 10 minutes; discard the water.

Warm the oil in a large stockpot over medium heat and fry the green pepper, garlic, and then the onion. When the onion is translucent, add the beans, water, chicharron, and the rest of condiments, except for the salt. Cook covered, over medium to low heat until beans are soft, for 45-60 minutes. Remove the ginger.

Five minutes before serving, crack 1 egg into the soup per person, without stirring or mixing, to allow the eggs to cook whole. After 1-2 minutes, carefully stir the soup so as not to break the eggs. In a small bowl, whisk 2 more eggs and add to the soup, stirring, so they will mix in. Because the chicharron can be quite salty, taste the soup first before adding any more salt.

Add a dollop of sour cream to each bowl before serving

Serves 4-6.

Sopa de Frijoles Blancos (Navy White Bean Soup)

1 pound of dried white navy beans
1 small onion, chopped
1 garlic clove, minced
1 large tomato, diced
½ teaspoon of ground cumin
1 teaspoon of dried oregano
1 bay leaf

1 piece of peeled ginger, about 1½-inch long
salt and ground black pepper to taste
2 pounds of pig's feet, cut into pieces
4 carrots, peeled, cut
3 medium potatoes, peeled, cut
1 pound of *chicharron* (fried pork rind)
1 tablespoon of vegetable oil
6 cups of water
2 sprigs *culantro* (You can substitute mint.)

Soak the beans for about 2 hours in enough warm water to cover, or parboil them for 10 minutes; discard the water.

Heat the oil in large stockpot and fry the garlic, onion, carrots, tomato, and pig's feet. When browned, add the beans, water, condiments, potatoes, chicharron, and ginger. Cook covered, over medium heat. If boiling hard, turn the heat to low. Continue cooking for about 45-60 minutes. Because the chicharron can be quite salty, taste the soup first before adding any more salt.

By adding 2 Merguez or Polish sausages (kielbasa), cut into bite-size pieces, and by reducing the water as in a stew, this would become a Potaje, which is a Cuban dish.

Serves 4-6.

Sopa de Elote (Corn Soup)

4 ears of corn or two 14½ ounce cans of sweet corn
1 small onion, chopped
½ small red bell pepper, chopped
4 breasts of chicken, cubed
1 large tomato, diced
2 garlic cloves, minced
8 cups of water
salt and ground black pepper to taste

Husk the corn and remove the silk. In a medium pot, boil the corn for 5 minutes, adding a couple of pinches of salt after 3 minutes. Remove the kernels from 2 of the 4 ears of corn with a sharp knife, mash the kernels, and set the mashed and whole corn aside. Reserve the water.

In another saucepan, fry the garlic and red pepper, add the onion and tomato, and continue frying until soft. Add the chicken pieces and wait until they're brown. Slowly add the reserved water and continue cooking, covered, over medium to low heat for about 20 minutes. Add the mashed and whole corn and cook for another 10 minutes. Turn the heat off and let the soup sit before serving to gather flavor.

Serves 5-6.

Sopa de Rosquilla (Corn Ring Soup)

To Make the Rings:

1 cup of masa harina
¼ pound of *sincho* cheese, ground, or 1½ cup of grated parmesan cheese
2 tablespoons of soft butter
1 garlic clove, minced
1 teaspoon of *achiote* paste
¼ cup of water
salt and ground black pepper to taste
½ cup of vegetable oil, for frying

In a large bowl, thoroughly mix all of the above ingredients except the oil. Shape the dough into rings (1½-inch diameter). In a deep skillet, heat the oil and fry the rings until golden brown. Remove and set aside on a paper towel to drain.

For the Soup:

Two 14½-ounce cans of chicken stock
½ cup of onion, finely chopped
1 garlic clove, minced
1 large tomato, diced
¼ cup of red bell pepper, chopped
2 cups of milk
2 eggs, beaten
4 mint sprigs or cilantro sprigs

Take a couple of teaspoons of the dough and dissolve in the milk. Heat the chicken stock, adding the thickened milk slowly to it while stirring.

In the reserved oil, fry the pepper, garlic, and onion. When the onion is translucent, add the tomatoes and fry until soft. Add to the chicken broth together with the rings and the mint. Stir all of the ingredients together, bring to a slow boil, and simmer over low heat for about 30 minutes. Slowly add the beaten eggs into the soup. Continue cooking for another 10 minutes. Season with salt and ground black pepper.

Garnish with fried onions, when serving, or additional fried corn rings.

Serves 6.

Gazpacho

2 medium zucchini, peeled, seeded (reserve ¼ cup of chopped
     zucchini for garnish)
1 small cucumber, peeled, seeded
1 medium green bell pepper, seeded
1 small onion, quartered
1 small garlic clove
3 large tomatoes, peeled, seeded

2 tablespoons of red-wine vinegar
1 teaspoon of Worcestershire sauce
¼ teaspoon of chopped serrano pepper or hot pepper sauce to taste
1-1½ cups of water, or tomato juice (I often use V-8 juice.)
salt and ground black pepper to taste

Combine all the ingredients in a food processor or blender, except the ¼ cup of reserved zucchini, and process to a liquid consistency. Refrigerate until ready to eat, or serve at once, adding the chopped zucchini as garnish. Perfect for a hot summer day.

Serves 4-5.

Sopa de Papas Dulce con Plátanos Maduros (Sweet Potato and Yellow Plantain Soup)

2 large sweet potatoes, peeled, cut up
½ teaspoon of dried basil leaves, crushed
2 ripe yellow plantains, peeled, cut up
2 tablespoons of olive oil
1 small onion, quartered
1 medium garlic clove, minced
2 slices ginger, peeled,
salt and ground black pepper to taste
three 14½-ounce cans of chicken stock
2 cups of water
¼ teaspoon of nutmeg
½ teaspoon of cumin
8 ounces of sour cream or yogurt
8 chive sprigs, chopped fine, for garnish

In a medium saucepan, heat the oil and fry the garlic, followed by the onion; when translucent, add the sweet potatoes and continue frying for about a minute. Add the plantains and sauté them for a few minutes. Add the water and bring to a soft boil. Cook the vegetables for about 10 minutes.

Meanwhile in a medium bowl, dissolve the sour cream in the chicken broth; add it to the vegetables together with the ginger. Season with the salt, black pepper, thyme, cumin, and nutmeg. Continue cooking until both vegetables are very soft. Blend in a food processor or blender until liquid. Serve hot.

Serves 6.

Sopa de Pollo (Chicken Soup)

1 whole chicken, cut up
1 medium onion, chopped
2 garlic cloves, chopped
½ cup of red bell pepper, chopped
2 carrots, peeled, cut up
2 potatoes, peeled, cubed
2 chayotes, peeled, seeded, cubed
5 mint sprigs
2 medium tomatoes, chopped, seeded
3 tablespoons of vegetable oil
½ teaspoon of ground cumin
1 teaspoon of basil
juice of 2 limes
salt and ground black pepper to taste
1 teaspoon of serrano pepper, finely chopped
6-8 cups of water

In large pan over medium heat, sauté the garlic, sweet bell pepper, and onions until soft and translucent. Add the cut-up chicken and fry it until light golden. Add in the water with the rest of the condiments. Bring to a boil. Reduce the heat and simmer for about 30 minutes. Add the vegetables to the soup and cook for about 20-25 minutes more, or until the vegetables are tender and ready to eat. Turn off heat and let sit for about 20 minutes before serving to gather flavor.

Serves 5-6.

Sopa de Tortilla (Tortilla Soup)

2 tablespoons of vegetable oil
2 garlic cloves, minced
5 cilantro sprigs, chopped
1 medium onion, chopped
3 medium tomatoes, chopped
2 breasts of chicken
3 cups of water
two 14½-ounce cans of chicken stock
½ teaspoon of ground cumin
1 teaspoon of jalapeño pepper, chopped
1 bay leaf
1 teaspoon of basil
salt and ground black pepper to taste
juice of 1 lime
4 tortillas, thinly sliced (shoestring style)
¼ cup of vegetable oil, for frying the tortillas

Sauté the garlic, onion, tomatoes, and jalapeño in a large saucepan over medium heat until soft. Add the chicken and fry until light golden brown. Add the rest of the ingredients, except the tortillas. Bring to a boil; reduce the heat and simmer for about 40-50 minutes. Remove the chicken breasts from the soup and let them cool. Shred the breasts and return to the soup.

In a large frying pan, heat the vegetable oil until hot, fry the sliced tortillas until golden brown. Remove, place on a paper towel to drain, and sprinkle them with salt. When ready to serve, garnish each bowl with a handful of tortilla strips.

Serves 6.

Sopa de Pescado (Fish Soup)

5 whole, firm-fleshed fish, cut in halves (with the heads and tails
    left on)
1 garlic clove, minced
1 small onion, sliced
¼ cup of red bell pepper, chopped
¼ cup of green bell pepper, chopped
2 medium tomatoes, peeled, seeded, sliced
2 tablespoons of butter
pinch of sugar
1 teaspoon of *achiote* paste
5 cups of milk
3 cups of water
2 large carrots, peeled, cut in bite sizes
2 potatoes, peeled, cubed
2 chayotes, peeled, cubed
2-3 teaspoons of white flour for thickening
3 *culantro* leaves
salt and ground black pepper to taste

This dish is mostly served on Fridays during Lent. Grandmother
would also make Crab Soup following this recipe, using about
10 whole local crabs, which, in Nicaragua, are about the size of
blue crabs.

In a large saucepan over medium heat, melt the butter and fry
the peppers, garlic, and onion until soft. Add the water and bring
to a slow boil; add the fish halves with the heads attached, salt,
tomatoes, annatto paste, and culantro. Let cook, simmering, for
about 30 minutes.

Dissolve the flour in 1 cup of milk until smooth; slowly add it
to the water while stirring. Add the rest of the milk, the fish
halves with the tails attached, sugar, potatoes, chayotes, and carrots.
Simmer for another 30 minutes, stirring often to avoid burning

the bottom of the pan. The soup is done when the fish is flaky and the vegetables are soft. Let sit for about 20 minutes to gather flavor.

Serves 8.

Sopa de Almejas (Clam Chowder)

16-18 medium clams in their shells
1 filet of firm-fleshed fish (12 ounces), cubed (I've used whitefish.)
1 medium onion, peeled, chopped
2 large carrots, peeled, diced
3 medium potatoes, peeled, cubed
2 garlic cloves, peeled, minced
2 cups of milk
1 cup of water
2 tablespoons of flour
2 tablespoons of olive oil
salt and ground black pepper to taste
½ teaspoon of *achiote* paste (Yes, my grandmother used it even in seafood dishes.)
dill (to garnish)

Scrub the clams with a vegetable brush until thoroughly clean. Place 1 cup of water in a large stockpot and add the clams. Cover and bring to a boil over medium-high heat; turn the heat to low and steam the clams for 4-5 minutes. Decant the clam liquid into a bowl and save, being careful not to include any sand. Remove the clams from the shells and dice them. Discard any that do not open. (You can also use canned clams without the shells, in which case, substitute bottled clam juice for the clam liquid.)

Heat the oil in a saucepan over medium heat and fry the garlic and onions until soft. Add the fish and clams, and fry until lightly golden. Combine the potatoes and carrots with the fish. Add the water from the clams (or a bottle of clam juice) and 1 cup of the milk. Cover and bring to a slow boil on medium-low heat. Simmer for about 30 minutes.

Dissolve the flour and achiote in 1 cup of milk; slowly add it to the soup, stirring until the soup gets thickened. If too thickened, add a little bit of milk. Add salt and black pepper.

Garnish with dill.

Serves 4.

Sopa de Maiz (Corn Chowder)

3 ears of corn, kernels removed (substitute with one can [15¼-
  ounces] of whole sweet corn)
1 small onion, peeled, chopped
1 large carrot, peeled, diced
1 medium potato, peeled, diced small
1 garlic clove, peeled crushed
¼ cup of green bell pepper, chopped
one 14½-ounce can of chicken stock
1 cup of milk
1 tablespoon of flour
2 tablespoons of olive oil
1 teaspoon of butter
salt and ground black pepper to taste
5 cilantro sprigs, chopped

Heat the oil and the butter in a saucepan over medium-high heat. Fry the green pepper, onion, and garlic until soft, and then add the potatoes, carrots, and corn. Continue frying for about 20 seconds. Slowly add the chicken stock, and cover. Bring to a slow boil on medium-low heat. Simmer for about 30 minutes.

In a small container, dissolve the flour in the cup of milk. While the soup is still simmering, slowly add the milk mixture to the saucepan, stirring until the soup becomes thickened. If too thickened, add a little bit of milk. Add salt and black pepper to taste. Garnish with chopped cilantro

Serves 4.

Sopa de Tomate (Tomato Soup)

3 large tomatoes, peeled, seeded (or 1 [14½-ounces] of tomato
    soup)
1 small onion, chopped
2 eggs
½ teaspoon of serrano pepper (or Tabasco sauce to taste)
salt and ground black pepper to taste
1 cup of water
2 tablespoons of olive oil
½ teaspoon of Worcestershire sauce

This soup is frequently offered as a hangover cure.

Blend the tomatoes and water in a food processor or blender. In a medium saucepan, heat the oil and fry the onion and serrano pepper. When the onion is translucent, add the tomato mixture and bring to a slow boil, stirring often. After 15 minutes, beat 1 egg and stir it in the soup; wait 2 minutes and then crack the other egg whole into the soup; cook until soft hard boiled. Add the Worcestershire, salt, and pepper to taste. Serve hot.

Serves 2.

Sopa de Zanahoria con Maduro (Carrot and Plantain Soup)

1 tablespoon of vegetable oil
1 medium sweet onion, chopped
2 garlic cloves, minced

½ teaspoon of jalapeño pepper, seeded, minced
1 pound of carrot, peeled, cut up
2 ginger slices
1 cup of water
4 cups of chicken stock
1 ripe yellow plantain, peeled, quartered
½ teaspoon of honey
½ teaspoon of ground cumin
¼ cup of cilantro leaves, to garnish
¼ cup of sour cream
¾ cup of yogurt
pinch of sugar
7 chive sprigs, chopped (or cilantro)
1 tablespoon of peanut oil
salt and ground black pepper to taste

Heat the oil in a medium saucepan over medium-high heat and fry the onion, garlic, ginger slices, and jalapeño, until the onion is soft and translucent. Add the carrots, water, chicken stock, honey, cilantro, and cumin. Heat to boil, and then simmer, covered, for 10 minutes. Add the plantain and continue simmering for another 20 minutes or until vegetables are soft.

Remove from heat and let cool for a few minutes. Purée in blender or food processor until smooth. Return to pot. If soup is too thick, add chicken stock as needed; adjust seasonings.

In a medium bowl, mix the yogurt, sour cream, peanut oil, chives, salt, and pepper to taste. When ready to serve, add a dollop of the mixture to each bowl.

Serves 4-5.

Sopa de Albondigas (Meatball Soup)

½ cup of masa harina
1 pound of lean pork loin
2 pounds of pork ribs
2 large eggs, lightly beaten
1 cup breadcrumb, finely ground
2 medium onions, sliced
½ cup of green bell pepper, seeded, sliced
1 teaspoon of *achiote* paste
¼ teaspoon of oregano
½ teaspoon of cumin
4 cups of water
salt and ground black pepper to taste
20 mint leaves

In a large stockpot, put the pork loin, ribs, black pepper, 1 sliced onion, half of the sliced green bell pepper, 10 mint leaves, and water. Bring to a boil and cook on medium-low heat for about 30 minutes. Remove the loin and continue simmering over low heat.

In a food processor or blender, chop the pork loin into small pieces together with the rest of the onion, green pepper, mint leaves, oregano, and cumin. In a large bowl, mix the meat with the masa harina, breadcrumbs, annatto paste, salt, and black ground pepper. Then, fold in the eggs, making sure everything is well covered.

Make ping-pong-sized balls with the meat mixture, and gently place them in the simmering broth with a slotted spoon, being careful not to break them. Continue cooking over low heat for another 20-30 minutes; serve hot.

Serves 8.

VEGETABLES

Berenjena con Maduro (Eggplant with Plantain)

3 medium eggplants, sliced
2 ripe large yellow plantains
1 small chopped onion
¼ cup of green bell pepper, chopped
1 garlic clove, minced
1 large tomato, chopped
4 tablespoons of vegetable oil
½ cup of cilantro sprigs, chopped
1 cup of fresh sweet whole corn
salt and ground black pepper to taste

Wash and cut the eggplants lengthwise into 4-5 slices each. Place on paper towel, sprinkle with salt and leave to drain. (Eggplants are watery; the salt will help in removing more of the excess water.) Meanwhile, peel the plantains and slice them.

Heat the oil in a skillet and fry the plantains until golden brown. Remove and put aside. Squeeze the eggplants to remove any excess water. In the same skillet where you fried the plantains, fry the eggplants until golden brown. Remove and set aside. Now fry the green pepper, garlic, and onion in the same skillet, until the onion is soft and translucent; add the tomatoes and continue cooking until soft.

In a lightly oiled baking dish, place the slices of eggplants first, followed by the slices of plantains, the mixture of onions, green peppers, tomatoes, and the corn. Bake covered for 15-20 minutes at 300°F.

Sprinkle with chopped cilantro before serving.

Serves 4-5.

Puré de Plátano (Mashed Plantain)

3 large green plantains
1 large garlic clove, whole
¼ cup of sweet onion, chopped
2 cups of water

Known also in some Hispanic countries as Fufu and Mofongo. Cut and peel the plantains. Place them in a saucepan together with all of the above ingredients. Bring to a boil and cook covered over medium heat until plantains are soft, about 20 minutes. Remove and let cool.

Then:

2 medium tomatoes, seeded
1 medium sweet onion, quartered
2 small garlic cloves, minced
1 can (14½-ounces) of chicken stock
½ cup of cilantro
salt and ground black pepper to taste
1 teaspoon of serrano pepper, seeded (optional)
1 cup of *chicharron* (fried pork rind)
1 teaspoon of *achiote* paste
juice of 2 limes

In a blender or food processor, add the plantain and 1 cup of chicken stock. Chop fine. Add the tomatoes, onion, garlic, fried pork rind, cilantro, salt, black pepper, and serrano pepper. Continue chopping until only tiny pieces are left.

In a small bowl, dilute the achiote paste with the lime juices. Add it to the plantain mixture. Mix everything thoroughly; add more salt and stock, if needed. Place in a serving dish. Serve at room temperature. Can be made a couple of days ahead and kept refrigerated.

Serves 6-8.

Guiso de Pipian (Squash Stew)

4 pale green squash
3 tablespoons of vegetable oil
3 slices of bread, without crust
1 cup of milk
1 egg, beaten
1 tablespoon of soft butter
1 small onion, finely chopped
1 garlic clove, minced
¼ cup of green bell pepper, chopped
2 large tomatoes, quartered
¼ teaspoon of cumin
½ teaspoon of basil
¼ cup of water
salt and black pepper to taste
¼ cup sour cream

The squash is found at the Mexican markets, or substitute patty pan or chayote squash.

In a medium bowl, soak the bread in the milk, until the bread is soft. Meanwhile, rinse the squash, trim the ends, and cut in cubes. In a saucepan, heat the oil and fry the garlic, green pepper, and onions until soft and translucent. Mix in the squash, butter, and tomatoes. Add the water and cook covered on low heat for about 15 minutes. If using patty pan squash, cook for 20 minutes.

Thoroughly mix the soaked bread with an electric beater. Add the sour cream, egg, salt, black pepper, basil, and cumin; blend. Slowly add this mixture to the squash, stirring, to mix all of the ingredients together. Cook for another 20-30 minutes, or until squash is tender, stirring at intervals.

Serves 4.

Guiso de Maiz con Chayote (Corn and Chayote Stew)

1 cup of fresh corn, cut from the cob, or 1 can (15¼-ounces) of whole kernels
1 medium onion, sliced
2 garlic cloves, crushed
2 tablespoons of butter
3 chayotes, peeled, seeded, cubed
1 large tomato, seeded, sliced
¼ cup of yellow bell pepper, sliced
½ cup of half-and-half
1 tablespoon of white flour for thickening
1 tablespoon of breadcrumbs
¼ cup of chicken stock
5 cilantro sprigs, chopped
salt and ground black pepper to taste
pinch of sugar

In a medium saucepan over moderate heat, fry the garlic, yellow pepper, and onion in butter until translucent. Add the corn kernels, tomatoes, and chayotes and stir-fry for 1 minute. Pour in the chicken stock. Cover. Cook on low heat for 15 minutes to soften the vegetables.

Dilute the flour in the half-and-half and add it to the chayotes with the salt, breadcrumbs, sugar, and cilantro. Simmer over low heat for about 15-20 minutes to ensure that the flavors have combined and the chayote is soft.

Serves 6.

Chilotes Con Crema (Baby Corn with Cream)

20 ears of baby corn
1 cup of sour cream
2 tablespoons of butter
salt and ground black pepper to taste
1 small onion, sliced
½ cup of green bell pepper, chopped
1 garlic clove, minced
½ cup of milk
¼ cup of mint

You can find jars of ready-to-eat baby corn in the specialty areas of many supermarkets.

Fry the green pepper, onion, and garlic in the butter in a medium saucepan over medium heat. Add the corn, salt, black pepper, and mint. Mix the milk with the sour cream; add it to the corn, stirring, to mix it thoroughly. Cook covered for 12-15 minutes, stirring often, so it doesn't stick to the pan. Turn off the heat and let sit for about 10 minutes before serving to gather flavor.

Serves 4-6.

Guiso de Chilote (Baby Corn Stew)

20 ears of baby corn, cut in half
8 ounces of butter
1 cup of half-and-half
2 eggs

1 tablespoon of breadcrumbs
1 medium onion, chopped
¼ cup of red bell pepper, chopped
salt and ground black pepper to taste
¼ cup of cilantro

In a medium saucepan, fry the corn in the butter together with the red pepper and the onion. When the onion is soft, add the cilantro, milk, breadcrumbs, salt, and black pepper. Cook over low heat for about 12 minutes. Whisk the eggs; slowly add them to the corn. Stir and let cook 5-6 more minutes before serving.

Serves 6.

Fritura de Plátanos (Plantain Fritters)

3 dark green plantains, skinned and halved
1 cup of water
1 very ripe yellow-black plantain
¼ cup of white flour
1 egg, beaten
¼ cup of cilantro
salt and ground black pepper to taste
pinch of sugar
½ cup of vegetable oil

Put the green plantains in a medium saucepan with the water and cook covered over medium heat for about 20 minutes or until soft. Remove and let cool. Reserve the water.

Remove the skin from the yellow plantain, place in a blender or food processor together with the boiled green plantains, ¼ cup of the reserved water, salt, cilantro, sugar, and the white flour. Blend until smooth. Add the egg and continue blending until you obtain a custard-like consistency; if the mixture is too dry, add more water.

In a large frying pan, heat the oil. With a spoon, drop some of the dough in the frying pan—about the size of a cookie. Flatten it with a spatula on both sides. Remove the fritters from the pan and place them on a paper towel to drain. Serve warm, accompanied by sour cream.

Makes about 14-16 servings.

Puré de Papas (Mashed Potatoes)

2 pounds of white or red potatoes
2 garlic cloves, minced
½ cup of whole warm milk
3 tablespoons of butter, softened
$1/3$ cup of sour cream, at room temperature
½ medium onion, sliced
salt and ground black pepper to taste
½ teaspoon of paprika
2 tablespoons of chopped mint
4 cups of salted water

Place 4 cups of cold, salted water in a large pan, add the potatoes with their skins, a garlic clove, and the onion. Bring to a slow boil. Cook for about 30 minutes, until potatoes are soft. Drain, let cool, and peel.

In a large bowl, mash the potatoes and mix in the milk, butter, and sour cream until thoroughly blended. Add the minced garlic, salt, pepper, and paprika, and continue mashing until well mixed.

Sprinkle with mint just before serving.

Serves 6-8.

Puré de Malanga (Taro Root Purée)

6 *malangas*
1 garlic clove, minced
1½ cups of chicken stock, warm (or substitute milk with 2 table-
    spoons of butter)
½ medium onion, sliced
salt and ground black pepper to taste
4 cups of salted water

This dish is given to babies, when they are beginning to eat solid
food. When my daughters were little, they loved it. The only
way they could remember to ask for it was to call it "the mush."

Peel the taros with a potato peeler. Place in a medium saucepan with
the salted water and sliced onion; bring to a boil and cook for about
20 minutes until the taros are soft. Drain and let them cool.

In a large bowl, mash the taros with a potato masher. (Do not
use a blender, as this makes the taro gummy.) Combine the stock
with the minced garlic; slowly pour the stock in the malanga
purée and continue mixing. Add salt and pepper to taste.

Another variation is to add cooked chicken breasts and carrots,
chopped finely; or better yet, make it with leftover chicken, beef
soups, or stews.

Serves 4.

SALADS

Ensalada de Frijoles Rojos (Red Bean Salad)

1 tablespoon of olive oil
½ tablespoon of apple cider vinegar
2 tablespoons of water
1½ cup of red beans, rinsed, drained
1 small onion, chopped
1 medium tomato, chopped
1 garlic clove, minced
1 medium carrot, peeled, cooked al dente, diced small
1 medium beet, cooked al dente, chopped small
½ teaspoon of serrano pepper, finely chopped
½ cup of cilantro, chopped
salt and ground black pepper to taste
1 small (8-ounces) of whole sweet corn, drained

(You can substitute a mayonnaise and mustard mixture for the olive oil, vinegar, and water.)

Combine all of the above ingredients and chill before serving.

Serves 4-5.

Ensalada de Repollo (Cabbage Salad)

½ head of white cabbage, shredded
juice of 1 lime
2 large tomatoes, finely diced

2 tablespoons of white vinegar
6 *congo* peppers, mashed
¼ cup of water
salt and ground black pepper to taste

Mix everything together, adding as much of the mashed congo peppers as you can stand.

Serves 5-6.

Ensalada de Lechuga (Iceberg Lettuce Salad)

1 small head iceberg lettuce
2 large carrots, peeled
2 large beets, boiled soft, peeled
2 large ripe tomatoes
1 medium red onion
10 large radishes
2 tablespoons of white vinegar
¼ cup of water
salt and ground black pepper to taste
½ teaspoon of serrano pepper

Discard any wilted outer leaves of the lettuce. Arrange the remaining leaves around a large serving dish. Slice the vegetables. Place the tomatoes on top of the lettuce, followed by the beets, onions, carrots, and radish, in layers. In a small container, mix the water with the white vinegar, salt, black pepper, and serrano pepper; pour over the vegetables and serve.

Serves 5-6.

Ensalada de Papas (Garlic Potato Salad)

3 pounds of white or red potatoes
3 garlic cloves, minced

1 teaspoon of Dijon mustard
2 tablespoons of sherry vinegar
¼ cup of olive oil
10 green pimento-stuffed olives, sliced
1 small onion, sliced
½ cup of cilantro, chopped
salt and ground black pepper to taste
2 cups of salted water

Put the unpeeled potatoes and sliced onion in salted water; cook until soft. Drain. Peel and dice the potatoes. Place in a medium bowl and mix with the cilantro and green olives.

In a small bowl, whisk together the mustard, vinegar, oil, salt, and black pepper. Add the dressing to the potatoes, tossing them together until well covered. Adjust seasoning to taste. Sprinkle some cilantro on top before serving.

Serves 6.

Main Dishes

Gallina Rellena (Stuffed Hen)

Traditionally, this dish is prepared for Christmas dinner, which is served at around 1 AM on December 25, after everyone has returned from midnight mass. Instead of Santa Claus, Baby Jesus arrives after the children have gone to sleep, leaving presents on and around their beds.

Stuffing

4 tablespoons of bread stuffing
4 tablespoons of *salsa Inglesa* (Worcestershire sauce)
8 tablespoons of milk
½ tablespoon of red wine
3 pounds of ground pork
4 ounces of prunes, cut in quarters
4 eggs
4 ounces of raisins
4 medium onions, chopped
2 tablespoons of capers
2 garlic cloves, minced
¼ cup of walnuts
¼ pound of melted butter
4 tablespoons of vegetable oil
4 tablespoons of sugar
½ teaspoon of salt and ground black pepper

One Day Before:

Soak the bread in milk until soft. Mix the ground pork with the eggs, Worcestershire sauce, wine, onions, garlic, butter, and sugar. Add the bread in milk, salt, and black pepper; mix thoroughly.

In a large frying pan, heat the oil and cook the above mixture until the pork is browned. If the mixture becomes too dry, add more milk and butter. It should be slightly moist and sweet. Two minutes before turning the burner off, add the raisins, prunes, walnuts, and capers; stir and mix well. Overall cooking time is about 7 minutes. Reserve for stuffing the hen.

The Next Day:

1 hen, 6-7 pounds (or 10-12 pounds of turkey)
2 garlic cloves, minced
juice of 2 limes
salt and ground black pepper to taste

Heat oven to 400°F.

Wash the hen thoroughly in cold water; pat dry. Salt and pepper the inside cavity well and rub the hen inside and out with the juice of 2 limes combined with the garlic.

Stuff the hen with the prepared mixture. Place in the oven and cook at 375°F for about 2-3 hours. If substituting a turkey, follow the accompanying directions for cooking it.

Serves 8-10.

Plato de Tortuga (Turtle Dish)

Turtle is a typical dish from Nicaragua, eaten most often during the Lenten season. Grandma would get up very early in the morning to mix all of the ingredients on her faithful grinding stone. The smells of garlic, annatto, and onion in the air were out of this world. She would then cook the turtle, stirring constantly. It's such a delicious, mouth-watering dish that neighbors would call on the house every Friday during Lent to see if Grandma was cooking turtle and if they could buy a serving (which Grandma might allow, depending on the circumstances).

Now with the cooperative in place for the conservation of endangered species, and with turtles and iguanas approaching extinction, only a limited number are legally available for cooking during the season. When I have been back home during Easter week, the smells of turtle and iguana, cooking in the market, transport me back to my childhood.

For Turtle

1 turtle, 15 pounds (or substitute 5 pounds of alligator meat, which is sometimes available, frozen in specialty markets)
4 lemons or 3 grapefruits
3 garlic cloves, peeled, minced
2 small onions, peeled, quartered
3 bay leaves
½ medium green bell pepper, sliced
1 cup of water
1 teaspoon of annatto paste
½ teaspoon of cumin
1 teaspoon of basil
1 teaspoon of oregano
½ teaspoon of salt and ground black pepper

When I was about 6-7 years old, I remember one of my uncles would kill a turtle by cutting the head off and hanging it upside down to drain the blood. Then, he would skin it with a very sharp knife while cutting the meat from the shell all around. I recalled this procedure so vividly that many years later, I was able to walk my husband through the whole process, after he shot a snapping turtle on our property in Georgia.

Wash the turtle pieces in cold water. Squeeze the lemon juices all over the meat and rub in well. Rinse. Place the turtle meat in a large bowl of fresh cold water with the pieces of squeezed lemon; let soak for about 10 minutes.

In a large saucepan, fry the pepper, onions, garlic, and the turtle meat, browning on all sides. Add the water and the rest of the ingredients. Cook covered at medium-low heat for about 2 hours or until tender. Drain. Reserve the broth. Shred the meat using 2 forks and return to the saucepan without turning on the heat.

Sauce for Stew

juice of 2 lemons
3 garlic cloves, peeled, minced
2 medium onions, sliced
2 medium tomatoes, quartered
1 cup of milk
6 eggs
1 teaspoon of basil
3 tablespoons of vegetable oil
$1/3$ cup of bread crumbs
1 teaspoon of oregano
½ teaspoon of salt and ground black pepper

Set aside the eggs, breadcrumbs, and lemon juice. Mix the milk and the other ingredients together to make the sauce. Slowly add the eggs and blend well. Add the mixture to the meat in the saucepan and turn the heat to medium. When it starts to boil, turn the heat to low. Add the breadcrumbs slowly, while stirring, and then the lemon juice. If too dry, add a bit of the reserved broth. Add the salt and pepper. Simmer for about 90 minutes until tender, stirring often. Serve with Salsa Criolla on top.

Serves 5-6.

Pinol de Iguana (Iguana Stew)

4 cups of masa harina
1 black iguana with eggs (There is no substitute for Iguana!)
2 onions, sliced
2 green bell peppers, chopped
2 tomatoes, sliced
1 garlic clove, minced
8 *culantro* leaves (or cilantro sprigs)
4 cups of water
½ teaspoon of salt and ground black pepper
½ cup of sour orange (juice of 2 limes plus juice of 2 grapefruits)
3 tablespoons of vegetable oil

Cut off the head, make an incision in the abdomen, and remove the innards and any eggs of a female. Discard the innards. Wash the eggs in cold water and set aside. Rinse the body cavity in cold water. Cook the iguana on a charcoal grill for about 40 minutes, turning it over after 20 minutes. Remove from grill, let cool, and peel off the skin. Wash the iguana and its cavity with sour orange.

Cut the iguana in pieces. In a large saucepan, heat the oil and fry the garlic and onion until transparent. Add the iguana pieces, salt, black pepper, and the remaining water. Cook over medium heat, until the meat is tender, for about 30 minutes. Remove the saucepan from the heat and strip the meat from the bones, discarding them and leaving the meat in the saucepan.

Thoroughly mix the masa harina into the broth with the iguana. Put the saucepan back on the burner; add the remaining ingredients, except the eggs, and mix thoroughly. Continue cooking for about

45-60 minutes, stirring often, until the masa harina is blended smoothly into the sauce and any sandy texture has disappeared. Add more water if it becomes too dry. During the last 20-30 minutes of cooking, add the eggs in their shells to cook in the mixture.

Serve hot with the eggs and Salsa Sofrita on top of the iguana.

Like the turtle recipe, this typical Nicaraguan dish is also prepared primarily during the Lenten season.

Serves 6-8.

Vaho (Steamed Vegetables with Beef)

4-5 large plantain leaves (found in frozen section of Mexican markets)
4-5 pounds of beef brisket, cut in 3-inch pieces
3 ripe yellow plantains, cut in half (Do not remove the skin.)
2 green plantains, peeled, cut in half
3-4 pounds of cassava, peeled, cut in 3-inch pieces
3 tomatoes, sliced
2 medium onions, sliced
1 green bell pepper, seeded, sliced
2 garlic cloves, minced
1 teaspoon of salt
1 teaspoon of black pepper
1 cup of apple cider vinegar
¼ cup of sour orange
½ cup of water

This is a very typical dish from Nicaragua. At home, it is always served with white rice on the side and white cabbage salad. Because most Hispanics pronounce the letter *V* as a *B* sound, you will usually hear this dish called "Baho."

The night before cooking, put the meat in a large plastic bowl with the tomatoes, onions, green pepper, garlic, salt, black pepper, sour orange, and vinegar, mixing everything together. Leave uncovered for 2-3 hours before going to bed; then, cover and refrigerate overnight. (Traditionally, the meat is washed with sour orange, salted, and placed outside in the sun in a covered large bowl the day before cooking it, to intensify its flavor by rapid aging.)

The following day in a large stockpot, arrange 4-5 plantain leaves on the bottom of stockpot and vertically up the sides. Make sure the bottom and sides of the pot are covered with leaves. Immediately place the yellow plantains on the bottom leaves, followed by the green plantains, yucca, meat, onions, pepper tomatoes, and remaining vinegar sauce. Cover with more plantain leaves, add the water, and cook on medium heat until boiling starts; lower the heat and simmer for about 4-5 hours. If it gets dry, add more water. The Vaho should always be steaming. The meat becomes very tender as a result of the steaming and fully absorbs the flavor of the plantain leaves.

Serves about 6-8 persons.

Pescado Asado (Grilled Fish)

6 whole fish (red snapper ~12-inch long), gutted and scaled
2 teaspoons of salt
2 teaspoons of black pepper
3 teaspoons of lime juice
2 tablespoons of chopped dill

Scrape the fish from tail to head and along the sides to remove any leftover scales; rinse in cold water and pat dry with paper towels. With a sharp knife, make 3-4 shallow, vertical incisions on both sides of the fish. Rub the fish inside and out with the lime juice, salt, and black pepper mixed together. Leave the fish in the juice for about a quarter of an hour.

Turn the broiler or charcoal grill on. Cook the fish for 3 minutes on each side, being careful not to break it apart, when you flip it over.

Sprinkle with dill when ready to serve.

Serves 6.

Pescado Seco (Bacalao, Dried Salt Cod)

2 pounds of *bacalao* (dried salt cod)
2 tablespoons of vegetable oil
1 medium onion, sliced
1 small green bell pepper, chopped
1 garlic clove, crushed
3 tomatoes, seeded, sliced
juice of 2 limes
lots of water, for soaking and rinsing
½ teaspoon of chili powder or ½ teaspoon of jalapeño, seeded
    and chopped finely
½ teaspoon of black ground pepper
salt, if needed

Bacalao is available quite inexpensively at almost every Mexican market—either in wooden boxes or just hanging on a string. Much of the effort in preparing the bacalao is devoted to removing the excess salt that is used to preserve it. The evening before cooking, rinse off the bacalao in cold water and place in a large bowl with enough cold water to cover. Let soak for 2 hours, discard the water, rinse off the bacalao, and repeat the process. Leave the bacalao out on the counter in a bowl overnight, with enough water to cover it.

Next day, discard the water and rinse off the bacalao. Place it in a large pan with water to cover, bring to boil for 2-3 minutes, remove from heat, and discard the water. Repeat the process one more time before preparing the dish as follows:

Cut the bacalao into 1½-inch squares. In a large skillet, heat the oil and fry the green peppers, garlic, jalapeño, onion, juice of the 2 limes, black pepper, and tomatoes. Add the fish and fry until golden brown. Lower the heat, cover, and simmer for another 15-20 minutes; serve hot.

Do not add any salt as the cod will have plenty of its own, even though it has been rinsed off several times. If not, add salt to taste.

Serves 4.

Pescado Tapado (Fish Stew)

1½ pounds of filet of fish, grouper or a hardy fish, cut in half
3 carrots, peeled, cubed
1 pound potatoes, peeled, cubed
½ cup each of small red and green bell peppers, diced
3 garlic cloves, crushed
2 small onions, chopped
2 tomatoes, seeded, quartered
2 lemons
½ cup of cilantro, chopped
2 tablespoons of vegetable oil
2 tablespoons of white flour
2 cups of water
½ teaspoon of salt
½ teaspoon of black pepper
½ teaspoon of butter
2 tablespoons of vermouth

Clean the fish of any scales. Wash in cold water. Rub the fish with the juice of 1 lemon. Sprinkle some white flour over it. In a buttered medium saucepan, fry 2 garlic cloves, 1 onion, and half of both bell peppers. Place the fish in and fry until golden. Add the 2 cups of water. When it comes to a boil, cook for about 6 minutes. Take out the fish but keep the water. In the fish water, cook the carrots and potatoes until al dente. Remove the vegetables and let them cool. Continue boiling the fish water until reduced to about ½ cup.

In a frying pan, add the oil and fry the rest of the bell peppers, garlic, and onion, together with the vegetables, until these are golden brown. Place the fish back in the reduced watered pan and the vegetables, salt, ground black pepper, vermouth, lemon juice, and tomatoes. Sprinkle the cilantro on top of the fish. Cook covered, simmering for about 10-12 minutes.

Serves 6.

Pescado Frito (Fried Fish)

1 red snapper (1½-2 pounds), gutted and scaled
2 cups of fine breadcrumbs
½ teaspoon of salt
½ teaspoon of black pepper
juice of 1 lemon
¼ cup of vegetable oil

Wash the fish thoroughly in cold water, pat dry with paper towels, and make 2-3 shallow, vertical incisions on both sides. Squeeze the lemon juice all over the fish; sprinkle it with salt and pepper, and cover it with the breadcrumbs.

Heat the oil in a large frying pan over medium heat, when bubbly, fry the fish in enough oil to keep it from sticking to the pan—add more oil as needed. Carefully, flip the fish over to cook on the other side. Continue frying. The fish is done, when it is golden brown on both sides and begins to fall from the bones.

For the Sauce:

1 medium tomato, sliced
1 small onion, sliced
2 tablespoons of apple cider vinegar
1 teaspoon of mustard
½ teaspoon of serrano pepper
1 teaspoon of vegetable oil
salt and ground black pepper to taste

In another frying pan, heat the oil and cook the onion until transparent. Add the rest of the ingredients and continue cooking for about 5 more minutes.

Place the fish on a platter and cover with the hot sauce before serving.

Lake Nicaragua, at the foot of Granada where I was born, holds a variety of fish, including the delicious *Guapote* and *Mojarra*, neither of which I have ever found anywhere else.

Serves 2-3.

Chuletas de Puerco (Pork Chops)

4 thick large pork chops
juice of 2 limes
1 small onion, sliced
1 large garlic clove, minced
3 tablespoons of orange juice
½ teaspoon of *achiote* paste
2 tablespoons of vegetable oil
salt and ground black pepper to taste

In a bowl, mix the onion, garlic, lime juice, orange juice, achiote paste, black pepper, and salt; marinate the pork chops in this mixture for a couple of hours, turning them over every now and then.

Before frying, drain the pork chops and reserve the marinade. In a large skillet, fry the pork chops over medium heat for 3-4 minutes on each side. (Do not overcook; pork tastes best when still moist and very faintly pink inside.) Remove the chops, set aside, and keep warm. Pour off the liquid from the marinade and reserve; in the same skillet, fry the remaining marinade mixture; when the onions are soft, pour in the reserved liquid and fry on medium-high, until the liquid boils off. Place the residual onion mixture on top of the pork chops and serve.

Serves 4.

Lomo de Puerco (Fried Pork Cubes)

1-1½ pounds of boneless pork loin
1 small onion, sliced
1 garlic clove, minced
¼ cup of green bell pepper, sliced
1 large tomato, chopped
½ cup of water
2 teaspoons of vegetable oil
½ teaspoon of *achiote* paste
juice of 1 lime
1 teaspoon of salt
½ teaspoon of ground black pepper

Cut the pork in 1-inch cubes. Heat the oil in a saucepan and fry the peppers, garlic, and onions. Add the pork, tomato, achiote paste, lime juice, salt, and black pepper. Slowly pour in the water. Bring to a boil over moderate heat. Cook about 40 minutes, stirring frequently, until the water has evaporated and the pork is browned on all sides.

Serves 6.

Manuelitas (Crepes filled with Cheese)

1 cup of milk
1 cup of all-purpose white flour
2 eggs
1 teaspoon of sugar
8 ounces of queso *fresco* (You can substitute cottage cheese.)
8 ounces of *añejo* cheese (You can substitute cream cheese.)
3 tablespoons of sugar
pinch of salt
2 tablespoons of vegetable oil
¼ cup of confectioner's sugar

This dish is usually eaten as a main course in my country, served with salad and vegetables. However, due to its sweetness, my husband prefers it as a dessert.

In a medium bowl, combine the milk, flour, 1 pinch of salt, and 1 teaspoon of sugar. When well mixed, add the eggs, whisking for a few seconds. Do not overbeat or else the crepes will be dense and hard. (This is the same recipe we use for making thin pancakes/crepes for breakfast.)

Heat the oil in a medium skillet over moderate heat, until it just starts to bubble, spoon in some of the mixture to make the crepe. When the edges turn golden, flip over and cook the other side; remove and stack on a plate. Repeat until the batter is used up.

In a medium bowl, combine both cheeses, 3 tablespoons of sugar, and a pinch of salt; mix well. Sprinkle some confectioner's sugar on each crepe. Put 2-3 teaspoons of the cheese mixture over it. Fold and wrap both ends. Serve warm, sprinkled with confectioner's sugar.

Serves 4-6.

Indio Viejo (Shredded Beef with Tortillas)

1½ pounds of skirt or flank steak, cubed
2 cups of water
1 medium onion, sliced
1 garlic clove, minced
½ cup of green bell pepper, chopped
2 large tomatoes, cut up
3 tablespoons of vegetable oil
2 teaspoons of *achiote* paste
juice of 1 lemon
2 eggs
salt and ground black pepper to taste
1- to 2-day-old tortillas, diced, or 1 cup of masa harina
4 mint sprigs

You can also use beef brisket. In a medium saucepan, heat the oil and fry the green bell pepper, garlic, onion, and tomatoes. Add the meat to the mixture and continue frying until lightly brown. Slowly pour in the water and bring to a boil; simmer for about 1 hour over medium-low heat.

When the meat is tender, remove it from the liquid and reserve. Soak the tortillas in the broth for about 15-20 minutes. If using the masa harina, dissolve it in the broth. Holding a fork in each hand, shred the meat, while the tortillas are soaking. Process the tortillas, broth, and achiote paste in a blender or food processor. Add the eggs, salt, black pepper, and process for another 30 seconds; return to the saucepan.

Add the remaining oil, the shredded meat, lemon juice, and the mint. Bring slowly to a boil, stirring often, to prevent burning. Cover and simmer for about 30-45 minutes.

Serves 5-6.

Pescozón (Squash Stuffed with Cheese)

4 large squash, pale green
4 ounces of *añejo* or *sincho* cheese, finely ground
2 eggs, separated
salt and ground black pepper to taste
5 tablespoons of vegetable oil
1 cup of water

Trim the ends of the squash. Put them with the water in a medium pot to boil for 15-20 minutes, or until soft. Remove. Cut the squash lengthwise and put on a plate to cool. Discard the water.

When the squash are cool, squeeze each piece between your hands to remove the excess water, which will cause the hot oil to splatter when frying the squash. Sprinkle salt and pepper on the inside of each squash. Spread 2 teaspoons of ground cheese over half of each squash and cover with the other half, until all the squash are stuffed.

Beat the egg white until high and fluffy, and then slowly add the egg yolks and a pinch of salt while continuing to beat. Cover the squash in the beaten egg mixture and fry in hot oil in a large skillet until golden brown. Remove and drain on paper towels; serve immediately.

Serves 4 pieces.

Repollo Relleno (Stuffed Cabbage)

10 cabbage leaves (Only white cabbage is available in my country.)
½ cup of vegetable oil
½ pound of ground beef, chicken, or pork
1 cup of plain-cooked rice
¼ cup of fine-chopped onion
1 garlic clove, chopped fine

2 tablespoons of chopped tomato
1 egg, separated
2 teaspoons of white flour
salt and ground black pepper to taste

Cut the thick center veins from the large leaves and discard them, leaving 2 halves. Use the small leaves whole. Cook the cabbage leaves in water over moderate heat for 2 minutes. Drain well and set aside.

Heat 2 tablespoons of oil in a skillet. Fry the meat until brown. Add the onion, garlic, salt, pepper, and tomatoes; fry until soft. Mix in the rice and cook for 1 more minute. Set aside.

Beat the egg white until stiff. Whisk the yolk lightly, and fold it in the egg white. Sift the flour and fold it in too.

Heat ¼ cup of oil in a skillet over medium heat. Place 1 tablespoon of the meat-rice stuffing on a cabbage leaf. Fold the leaf over diagonally to about 4-inch long and ½-inch thick. Dip the cabbage leaf in the egg mixture and place it in the frying pan. Brown both sides in the oil for about 2 minutes. Continue with the remaining leaves and meat-rice mixture. Drain on a paper towel and serve immediately.

Serves 6-8.

Carne Desmenuzada/Ropa Vieja
(Beef Threads/Old Clothes)

1½ pounds of skirt or flank steak, cut up in chunks
5 cups of water
3 tablespoons of vegetable oil
1 garlic clove, minced
1 medium onion, sliced
2 large tomatoes, sliced

½ green bell pepper, thinly sliced
2 tablespoons of sour orange juice
salt and ground black pepper to taste

Cook the beef in boiling water with ¼ of the sliced onion, ¼ of the green bell pepper, and salt over moderate heat until meat is tender. Remove and let cool. With a fork in each hand, pull the meat apart into 2- to 3-inch-long shreds.

Heat the oil in a skillet over medium heat. Fry the remainder green pepper for one minute; then add the onion, garlic, and tomatoes and fry till onion is soft. Add the shredded beef, black pepper, salt, and sour orange juice; mix well. Cover and simmer on low for about 12-15 minutes. Serve with plain white rice.

Serves 6.

Carne Tapada (Beef Stew)

1-2 pounds of stewing beef, cubed
1 medium onion, chopped
1 garlic clove, peeled, minced
¼ cup of green bell pepper, chopped
2 large tomatoes, seeded, quartered
2 tablespoons of vegetable oil
1 teaspoon of *achiote* paste
juice of 1 lemon
3 potatoes, peeled, cubed
2 large carrots, peeled, cut
1 teaspoon of oregano
¼ cup of pimento-stuffed green olives
1 teaspoon of cumin
salt and ground black pepper to taste
¼ cup of water
1 tablespoon of Worcestershire sauce
1 large chayote (optional)

In a small bowl, dissolve the achiote paste in the lemon juice. In a large saucepan, bring the oil to medium heat. Fry the garlic, green peppers, and onion until translucent. Add the meat and brown. Add the achiote-paste-lemon-juice mixture, tomatoes, oregano, cumin, and water; mix thoroughly. Cover and cook on medium-low heat for about 40 minutes. Add the vegetables, Worcestershire sauce, salt, and black pepper. If more juice is needed, add 2 tablespoons of water (or substitute white wine or vermouth). Continue simmering for another 20 minutes or until meat and vegetables are tender; serve hot.

Serves 6.

Tortillas Fritas con Tomates
(Fried Tortillas with Tomatoes)

1-day-old tortillas, cut in bite sizes
2 medium tomatoes, diced
1 small onion, chopped
¼ cup of green bell pepper, chopped
1 garlic clove, minced
1 cup of *chicharron* (fried pork rind pieces)
1 teaspoon of serrano, finely chopped
10 cilantro stems, chopped
juice of 1 lime
½ teaspoon of *achiote* paste
salt and ground black pepper to taste
2 tablespoons of vegetable oil

Heat the oil in a skillet and fry the green bell pepper, garlic, and onion. When the onion is translucent, add the tortillas, tomatoes, lime juice, chicharron, and remaining ingredients. Cook for about 10 minutes or until the chicharron is soft.

Serve as a main course with salad or as an appetizer.

Serves 5-6.

Carne Molida Tapada/Picadillo
(Ground Beef Stew)

3 tablespoons of vegetable oil
1 medium onion, diced
1 garlic clove, minced
¼ cup of green bell pepper, diced
1 pound of ground beef
½ teaspoon of ground cumin
½ teaspoon of oregano
2 medium tomatoes, seeded, chopped (or stewed tomatoes)
½ teaspoon of achiote paste
¼ cup of water
salt and ground black pepper to season
juice of 1 lime
3 large carrots, peeled, cubed
2 medium potatoes, peeled, cubed
2 tablespoons of red wine
½ cup of pimento-stuffed green olives, optional

Chayotes can substitute for potatoes. Heat the oil in a saucepan over medium heat. Fry the green bell pepper first followed by the onion until soft. Add the ground beef, and garlic. Cook until the meat is browned. Dilute the achiote paste in the lime juice. Add it to the meat, together with the spices, tomatoes, and water. Cover and cook for 30 minutes on medium-low heat. Add the vegetables and red wine. Cook for 20 minutes more or until vegetables are tender. Season with salt and black pepper.

Serves 6.

Hígado Frito (Fried Liver)

2 pounds of calf's liver steaks
1 medium onion, sliced
1 large tomato, sliced
1 garlic clove, minced

½ teaspoon of oregano
½ teaspoon of cumin
salt and ground black pepper to taste
1 cup of water
2 tablespoons of vegetable oil

In a medium saucepan, bring the liver, garlic, and half the onion to a boil in the cup of water. Cook for about 30 minutes. Remove the liver. Continue boiling the water until reduced to $1/8$ cup.

In a skillet, heat the oil until moderately hot, fry the liver with the rest of the onion, tomato, and other spices, stirring, as the liver is turning brown. When lightly browned, remove the liver to a serving dish. Add the reduced broth to the skillet with the onions and tomatoes. Raise the heat and fry until thickened; spoon over each piece of liver before serving.

Serves 4.

Variation: Instead of boiling, fry the liver steaks for about 2 minutes on each side until pink or to your liking. Keep warm. In the same skillet, fry the onions and tomatoes with the spices. When onions and tomatoes are soft, place them on top of the liver. Serve immediately.

Fricasé de Conejo (Rabbit Fricassee)

1 rabbit (2-3 pounds), cut up
¼ cup of red wine
1½ cups of chicken stock
4 garlic cloves, minced
1 small onion, chopped
1 bay leaf
½ teaspoon of oregano
1 teaspoon of thyme

juice of 1 lemon
2 small tomatoes, chopped
4 carrots, peeled, cubed
½ cup of green olives
3 tablespoons of vegetable oil
salt and ground black pepper to taste
½ cup of white flour

Rinse the rabbit pieces in cold water and pat dry with paper towels. Shake the rabbit pieces in a plastic back with the flour, salt, and pepper. In large saucepan, sauté the garlic and onion in vegetable oil; add the dredged rabbit pieces and lightly brown. Add the chicken stock, bay leaf, oregano, thyme, lemon, and tomatoes; mix together. Cook covered over medium-low heat for 3-4 hours. If boiling too hard, lower the heat to a simmer. Add the vegetables, green olives, and wine; continue simmering for another 30 minutes or until vegetables are soft. If too watery, uncover and cook on high heat for a couple of minutes to reduce the broth.

Serves 6.

Salpicón (Chopped Beef with Lime)

1½ pounds of chuck beef, rump roast, or even meaty soups' bones.
1 small onion, peeled, chopped
1 garlic clove, peeled, crushed
½ cup of green bell pepper, chopped
2 cups of water

Clean the meat of excess fat. In a medium saucepan, add all of the ingredients; bring to a boil. Lower the heat. Cover and simmer until the meat is tender (about 1½ hours). Remove from heat and let cool. Pour off the broth and freeze for use in soups later on.

In a food processor or blender, chop the meat until the pieces are very small (like ground beef). Place the meat in a bowl. Add the following ingredients and mix well:

1 small onion, finely chopped
2 large tomatoes, seeded, chopped finely
½ cup of finely chopped red bell pepper
juice of 3 limes
1 teaspoon of serrano pepper, chopped fine
8-10 cilantro sprigs, finely chopped
salt and ground black pepper to taste

When served cold, this is a refreshing dish for hot summer days.

Serves 4-5.

Leftover Salpicón makes a wonderful stuffing for Enchiladas, as follows:

Enchiladas (Stuffed Tortillas)

1 cup of cooked white rice
1½ cup of Salpicón, prepared as described above.
4 tortillas, homemade
2 eggs
salt and ground black pepper to taste
½ cup of vegetable oil
6 *congo* peppers, mashed
¼ cup of apple cider vinegar
¼ cup of water

This is also a good way to use day-old tortillas.

Combine the rice with the Salpicón. Cut the tortillas in half and fill them with the meat mixture, as if you were stuffing a pita bread. In a bowl, beat the egg whites until high and fluffy. Slowly add the egg yolks and a pinch of salt. Keep on beating. Dip the stuffed tortillas in the beaten eggs until covered. In a large skillet over medium heat, add the vegetable oil, and when moderately hot, fry the stuffed tortillas until golden brown. Remove and set aside.

In a bowl, mash the congo peppers and mix them with the vinegar and water. Add salt and black pepper to taste. Pour the sauce over the Enchiladas and serve.

Makes 8 pieces.

Pollo Tapado (Chicken Stew)

1 whole chicken, cut up
1 medium onion, peeled, cut
2 garlic cloves, peeled, minced
¼ cup of green bell pepper, chopped
2 large tomatoes, seeded, sliced
3 lemons
2 tablespoons of vegetable oil
1 teaspoon of oregano
1 teaspoon of *achiote* paste
3 potatoes, peeled, diced
3 large carrots, peeled, cubed
¼ cup of water
salt and ground black pepper to taste

Wash and rinse the chicken in cold water. Rub the juice of 2 lemons all over the chicken, inside and out. Set aside over paper towel to drain. Pat dry with a paper towel before cooking.

Heat the oil in large saucepan over medium. Fry the garlic, green pepper, and onion until translucent. Place in the chicken, brown lightly. Add the oregano, 1 lemon juice, achiote, tomatoes, and water. Cook on medium-low for about 30 minutes. Put in the vegetables; if too dry, add a bit of water. Stir. Cover. Simmer another 30 minutes, or until vegetables are tender.

Serves 6.

Arroz Aguado (Soft Rice with Chicken)

1 large chicken, cut up
2 small garlic cloves, peeled, minced
1 small onion, chopped
¼ cup of green bell pepper, chopped
2 ripe tomatoes, seeded, sliced
½ teaspoon of *achiote* paste
5 mint sprigs
½ teaspoon of oregano
1¼ cups of Arborio white rice
3 cups of water
salt and ground black pepper to taste
juice of 3 limes
2 chayotes, peeled, seeded, and cubed
3 large carrots, cut in bite size
2 tablespoons of vegetable oil
2 tablespoons of white wine or vermouth
½ cup of chicken stock

Wash the chicken thoroughly in cold water. Rub the chicken all over with ²/₃ of the lime juice. Set aside over paper towel to drain.

In a large saucepan, heat the oil and fry the bell pepper, garlic, onion, and tomatoes. When the onion is soft, add the chicken, and brown lightly all over. Add the water, oregano, mint, salt, and black pepper. Bring to a boil; lower the heat to medium-low. Add the rice. Dilute the achiote paste in the remaining lime juice; add it to the pan. Cook for about 40 minutes. If it is bubbling too hard, turn the heat to low. Stir. Place the vegetables and the white wine or vermouth in the pot. Continue cooking for another 20-25 minutes, until the vegetables are tender, the rice is soft and the chicken is coming apart. If too dry, add the chicken stock, if needed. The dish should resemble a risotto, only a bit more watery.

Adding 1 ripe bright yellow plantain, peeled and cut in 4 pieces, to the last 15-20 minutes of cooking, gives this dish a sweet flavor, which my husband likes very much.

Serves 6.

Arroz Aguado con Puerco (Soft Rice with Pork)

1½ pounds of pork loin, cut in 1½-inch squares
1½ pounds of pork ribs, cut up
2 small garlic cloves, peeled, crushed
1 small onion, chopped
¼ cup of green bell pepper, chopped
2 ripe tomatoes, seeded, sliced
½ teaspoon of *achiote* paste
4 *culantro* leaves, or 6 cilantro sprigs
½ teaspoon of oregano
½ teaspoon of cumin
1¼ cups of Arborio white rice
3 cups of water
salt and ground black pepper to taste
juice of 2 limes
3 chayotes, peeled, seeded, cubed
3 large carrots, peeled, cubed
2 tablespoons of vegetable oil
½ cup of chicken stock

In a large saucepan, heat the oil and sauté the bell pepper and garlic first, followed by the onion and tomatoes. When tomato is soft, add the pork pieces and brown all over. Add the rice, water, oregano, cumin, achiote paste, culantro, salt, and black pepper. Bring to a boil; lower the heat to medium-low. Cook for about 40 minutes.

If the rice is bubbling too hard, turn the heat to low. Stir. Place the chayotes and carrots in the pot; cook for another 20-25 minutes until the vegetables are tender. The dish should not be allowed to dry out—check it and add chicken stock when needed. Overall cooking time should be about 1 hour. The dish should resemble a risotto but with a slightly more watery consistency.

I have made this dish with only vegetables, and it is delicious. I use three 14½-ounce cans of vegetable stock, instead of water for added flavor.

Serves 6.

Lengua en Salsa de Tomate (Tongue in Tomato Sauce)

1 beef tongue (3-4 pounds)
juice of 2 lemons
½ medium green bell pepper, sliced
1 medium onion, sliced
3 large garlic cloves, crushed
2 bay leaves
3 cups of water

Rinse the tongue in cold water and place in a large pot with all the other ingredients. Cover, bring to a boil, and then lower the heat to medium-low, or low, if boiling too hard. Cook for 3 hours. Remove the tongue from the pot and let it cool, but continue boiling the broth, uncovered, until reduced to about ½ cup.

Remove the thick outer skin of the tongue by making a small incision in the skin, prying up the edge, and pulling it off. With a thin, sharp knife, I also carefully remove the top layer of the taste buds. Trim the fat and any bones from the back of the tongue. Cut the tongue in 1-inch cubes.

To Prepare:

½ cup of chopped red bell pepper
½ cup of chopped onion
2 garlic cloves, minced
2 large tomatoes, sliced
1 teaspoon of serrano pepper, chopped small
½ teaspoon of oregano
½ teaspoon of cumin
1 bay leaf
½ cup of reserved broth
salt and ground black pepper to taste
3 tablespoons of vegetable oil
3 large potatoes, peeled, cubed
¼ cup of red wine

Heat the olive oil in a large saucepan over medium heat. Fry the red pepper, garlic, onion, and tomatoes. Add the tongue and fry for a couple of minutes. Add the remaining ingredients, except the wine and potatoes. Mix together, cover, and continue cooking about 40 minutes. Turn the heat to low. Add the potatoes and cook another 15 minutes or until potatoes are tender. Add the wine and cook for 5 more minutes. If too watery, uncover the pan and cook for about 5 minutes to reduce the liquid.

Serves 5-6.

Lengua Fingida (False Tongue)

Meat Mixture:

1 pound of ground pork
1½ cups of masa harina

1 large egg
1 medium onion
1 small green bell pepper
1 large tomato
salt and ground black pepper to taste
1 garlic clove, mashed
10 mint sprigs
4 cups of water

This dish derives its name from the fact that ground pork meat is used, instead of beef tongue, and then shaped roughly in the form of a tongue before cooking.

Place the onion, green pepper, tomato, and mint in a blender and chop finely. Put this mixture in a large bowl. Add the masa harina, 1 egg, salt, black pepper, garlic, and the ground pork. Combine everything until well mixed.

Put the meat mixture in a cheesecloth and make a roll about 2 inches in diameter by about 8 inches in length; tie the ends with a string. Place it in a pan, add the water to cover, and bring to a boil. Cook covered on medium to low heat for about 40 minutes. Remove and let cool.

Sauce:

1 egg
1 large tomato, sliced, seeded
1 medium onion, sliced
1 garlic clove, minced
3 tablespoons of vegetable oil
salt and ground black pepper to taste
½ teaspoon of oregano

Unroll the cheesecloth and slice the meat into ¾-inch-wide pieces. Beat the egg and dip in the meat slices to cover both sides. Heat the oil in a skillet and fry the meat slices until lightly brown. Remove and in the same skillet, fry the tomato, onion, garlic, oregano, salt, and black pepper. When these are almost soft, put the meat slices back in the skillet. Simmer on low for about 7-10 minutes, spooning the sauce over the meat from time to time.

Serves 8.

Titiles/Mollejas (Chicken Gizzards)

2 pounds of chicken gizzards, cut in half
1 cup of water
4 garlic cloves, chopped
1 tablespoon of vegetable oil
1 teaspoon of *achiote* paste
juice of 1 lemon
1 small onion, chopped
1 large tomato, seeded, chopped
¾ cup of chopped red bell pepper
1 tablespoon of *salsa Inglesa* (Worcestershire sauce)
2 tablespoons of red wine
salt and ground black pepper to taste

In a small saucepan, heat the oil over medium heat. Fry the red pepper, garlic, and onion. When the onion is soft, add the gizzards. Continue frying for about 2 minutes until lightly brown. Cover and turn the heat to low.

In a very small bowl, dissolve the achiote paste in the lemon juice. Add it to the gizzards. Slowly add the water and chopped tomato. Simmer for about 40 minutes or until gizzards are tender. Add the Worcestershire sauce, salt, black pepper, and wine. If the gizzards are too watery at this point, continue cooking uncovered for 10 more minutes or until the juice is reduced.

This dish also makes an excellent appetizer.

Serves 6.

Pebre/Revolcado (Pork Stew)

Pork Meats:

3 tongues
2 kidneys
3 hearts
1 pound of boneless pork
2 pounds of liver
2 ears
8 cups of water
1½ teaspoons of salt
1 teaspoon of ground black pepper
juice of 3 lemons
1 small onion, sliced
2 garlic cloves, crushed
1 bay leaves

Remove the membrane of the tongue as per directions in Tongue in Tomato Sauce recipe. Save the water and continue cooking on low heat. Clean the hearts of any membranes and fat. Wash the remaining pork parts thoroughly in very cold water. Cover with the juice of 2 lemons and toss. Place in a large pot, add the water, onion, garlic, bay leaves, salt, and black pepper to taste, and cook over moderate heat for about 1 hour, or until the meats are tender.

Remove the meat, let cool, and cut into small cubes. Remove 2 cups of the broth and set aside. Return the diced meat to the broth and continue simmering, uncovered, while you make the sauce.

Sauce:

2 cups of sliced tomatoes
¼ cup of sliced onion

3 garlic cloves, crushed
½ cup of sliced red bell pepper
1 teaspoon of serrano pepper, finely chopped
¼ teaspoon of *achiote* paste
2 tortillas, quartered
½ cup of toasted bread crumbs
1 tablespoon of vegetable oil
½ teaspoon cumin
salt and ground black pepper to taste

In a deep medium saucepan over medium heat, fry the garlic, pepper, and onion. Add the remaining ingredients plus 2 cups of the reserved broth. Cook for 15-20 minutes. Set aside and let cool. When broth has cooled, put in a food processor or blender and process into a smooth sauce.

Add the sauce to the simmering meat and cook uncovered for 30 minutes over moderate to low heat, stirring frequently as the rich red sauce thickens. Adjust the salt. The sauce should be thick but not watery. Serve warm.

Serves 6-8.

Mondongo/Menudo Tapado (Tripe Stew)

3-4 pounds of honeycomb tripe, trimmed of fat
juice of 3 lemons (retain the squeezed lemons)
3 cups of cold water

This dish tastes best if cooked 1 or 2 days ahead, and reheated before serving.

Wash and rinse the tripe in cold water. Place in a bowl, cover with ²/₃ of the lemon juice, and mix thoroughly. (I often use grapefruit juice instead.) Add the cold water and the squeezed lemons. Set aside for 10 minutes. Rinse again. Put the tripe in a large pot with water and the remaining lemon juice. Boil for 20 minutes. Remove from burner. Cool. Discard the water. Rinse the tripe and the pot in cold water. Put the tripe back in the pot and add the following ingredients:

To Cook:

1 medium onion, sliced
2 garlic cloves, peeled, minced
¼ cup of chopped green bell pepper
1 large lemon
2 bay leaves
3 large carrots, peeled, cubed
2 cups of water

Bring the tripe and other ingredients to a boil. Lower the heat to medium-low. Cook covered for about 3 hours. Remove the tripe and let cool. Cut the tripe in 1-inch squares, and set aside. Reduce the broth over high heat, until there is only about ¼ cup left.

Sauce:

1 tablespoon of vegetable oil
1 garlic clove, peeled, minced
¼ cup of green bell pepper, chopped
1 small onion, chopped
1 large tomato, chopped
1 teaspoon of *achiote* paste
1 teaspoon of basil leaves
2 large potatoes, peeled, cubed
2 large carrots, peeled, cut up
2 tablespoons of vermouth or red wine
salt and ground black pepper to taste
½ teaspoon of oregano
the reduced broth

In large saucepan over medium heat, fry the green pepper first, followed by the garlic and onion; when the onion is translucent, add the tripe. Stir thoroughly, and then add the rest of the ingredients except for the wine. Simmer for about 1 hour. Add the wine and cook for another 15-20 minutes, until the broth thickens.

You can use chayote squash or yucca instead of potatoes. To add a delicate sweet taste to the tripe, cut in a ripe yellow plantain during the last 15-20 minutes of cooking.

Serves 4.

DESSERTS

Atolillo (Vanilla Custard)

1 quart of milk
5 tablespoons of cornstarch
7 tablespoons of sugar
1 egg yolk
2 cinnamon sticks
2 cloves
1 teaspoon of vanilla
1 ounce of raisins (optional)
dash of salt
cinnamon powder, to sprinkle

In a medium bowl, dissolve the cornstarch in ½ cup of milk until smooth. Beat in the egg yolk. When well mixed, force the mixture through a sieve or fine colander.

In a medium saucepan over medium heat, warm up the rest of the milk with the cinnamon sticks, sugar, cloves, vanilla, salt, and raisins. Slowly add the cornstarch mixture; bring to a boil. Turn the heat to low. Stir frequently until thickened and custard-like—about 10-15 minutes. Place in a large bowl or cake pan. Sprinkle cinnamon powder on top. Refrigerate and serve cold.

Serves 8.

Cajeta de Coco Blanco (White Coconut Custard)

4 cups of white rice
6 cups of water
¼ cup of dried coconut flakes
1½ cups of coconut milk
3 cups of sugar
1 cinnamon strip, 2-inch long
1 cup of milk

Soak the rice in 2 cups of water. Dissolve the sugar in the remainder 4 cups of water; add the dry coconut flakes, coconut milk, and the cinnamon. Cook over low heat, stirring often, for about 30 minutes.

Grind the rice in the milk and pass it through a sieve into the simmering coconut mixture. From this time on, stir continuously while cooking it for about another 30 minutes, or until it has the consistency of custard. Place on a rectangular oven pan, 9 x 12 inches, to cool. Cut in serving pieces.

Makes about 20-30 pieces.

Cajeta de Leche (Milk Custard)

8 cups of milk
4 cups of sugar
2 cups of rice
4 cinnamon sticks, 1-inch long

Soak the rice in 2 cups of milk for about 30 minutes or until soft. Put it in a blender, together with the milk, and grind. Over low heat, mix the rest of the milk, sugar, the rice-milk blend, and cinnamon sticks. Cook, stirring continuously, until the liquid is reduced to half, and the custard becomes a creamy dark color—be warned, this takes almost 2 hours! Pour into a square-cake pan and cut in pieces.

Makes about 20 pieces.

Cajeta de Manjar (Milk Brownies)

4 cups of white flour
4 cups of sugar
8 cups of milk
½ tablespoon of melted butter

Dissolve the flour in the milk; add the sugar and butter. Cook over low heat for about 2 hours, stirring often, until it has the consistency of a very thick custard. Pour over a greased cookie sheet. Cut in pieces.

Makes about 30 pieces.

Leche Burra (Caramel Candy)

1 quart of milk
4 ounces of melted butter
4 pounds of *piloncillo* (hard, brown sugar cane), ground
1 cup of vanilla
4 ounces of cocoa powder

In a medium saucepan, add the milk, ground piloncillo, and cocoa, stirring constantly, until the piloncillo has melted and the mixture has the consistency of custard. Slowly add the melted butter and vanilla; mix thoroughly. Remove from the heat and pour on a greased cookie sheet. Cut in small squares.

Makes about 50 pieces.

Ayote en Miel (Pumpkin in Syrup)

3 pounds of ground *piloncillo* (or brown sugar)
6 cups of water
4 cinnamon sticks, 2-inch long
6 cloves
3 pounds of pumpkin, 2-inch square

Over a slow heat in a saucepan, cook the ground piloncillo, cinnamon, water, and cloves. When boiling and the sugar has dissolved, put the pumpkin in, with the skin side facing up. Cover and simmer for 4-5 hours, or until all the liquid has evaporated and the pumpkin is resting on the bottom of the pan.

Makes about 12 pieces.

Almibar (Mango and Papaya Chutney)

2 dozens of small ripe mangoes, peeled
6 cinnamon sticks, 2-inch long
6 cups of water
4 cloves
6 cups of sugar
1 green papaya, peeled, seeded, cut in ¼ to ½-inch slices

It's very traditional in Nicaragua to also add an olive-sized fruit called Jocotes—these are unfortunately not available outside of Central America.

In large stockpot, dissolve the sugar in water; when it starts to boil, add the mangoes, cinnamon sticks, and cloves. Stir often. Remove the foam that keeps forming on top. Let the mangoes boil, uncovered, over medium heat for about an hour. Add the papaya slices and continue cooking for 2-3 hours, until light brown.

When cool, put in a large ceramic bowl or glass jar. Serve 1 mango with some papaya per person as dessert or as a snack. Can keep at room temperature for up to 15 days. Keeps longer in cool weather or in the refrigerator.

Sopa Borracha (Drunken Soup)

Marquesote *(resembles a pound cake)*

6 eggs
2 cups of flour
1½ cups of sugar
2 tablespoons of oil
½ lemon peel, grated
2 teaspoons of sweet sherry

Preheat the oven to 400°F. Beat the eggs until thickened and mayonnaise-like. Slowly add the sugar while beating until the mixture is fluffy. Add the flour, sherry, and the grated lemon; mix well. Pour in a greased mold of about 15 x 10 x 2 inches, and bake at 375°F for 12-15 minutes.

Syrup

2½ cups of sugar
4 cups of water
3 cinnamon sticks, 2-inch long
10 cloves
3 tablespoons of dark rum (or sweet sherry)
3 tablespoons of raisins (or 4 tablespoons of chopped prunes)

The night before preparing the dessert, leave the cinnamon sticks soaking in the dark rum or sherry. Over medium heat, boil the water and sugar until dissolved; add the cinnamon sticks and cloves. When the mixture begins to thicken, add the raisins. Continue boiling for another 5 minutes. Remove from heat and let cool. Force through a sieve. Add the cinnamon-flavored dark rum or sweet sherry; mix. Pour the syrup over the pound cake, making sure to soak it thoroughly. Decorate with the raisins or prunes.

Makes 20 pieces.

Pan Relleno (Stuffed Bread)

2 cups of white flour
1 cup of grated *sincho* cheese
1½ cups of milk
1 cup of sugar
⅓ cup of vegetable oil
2 eggs
pinch of salt

Preheat the oven to 375°F. Mix all the ingredients together. Grease an 8 x 12 inch oven pan, and put the mixture in it. Place the dish in the oven to bake for about 30 minutes, until an inserted toothpick comes out clean.

Serves 8-10.

Buñuelos (Cassava Patties with Syrup)

Patties

½ cup of long-grained rice
3 cups of shredded yucca
½ pound of *anejo* or *cotija* cheese, ground
½ teaspoon of sweet sherry (optional)
2 eggs
pinch of salt
½ cup of water
½ cup of vegetable oil for frying

Soak the rice in the water for 30 minutes to soften; grind it in a blender. Pass the rice through a sieve; discard the water. In a medium bowl and with an electric mixer, combine the rice and the rest of the ingredients until well blended. Take 1 tablespoon of the mixture and flatten into a small patty; continue until the mixture is used up.

Heat the oil in a large skillet. Put in several patties and fry both sides until golden brown. Remove and place on a paper towel to drain. Continue until all patties are fried; arrange a platter and serve, accompanied by the following sweet syrup:

Syrup

¾ cup of water
1 cup of sugar
3 tablespoons of brown sugar
2 cinnamon sticks, 2-inch long
6 cloves
1 fig leaf (optional, if available)

Over medium heat in a small pan, boil all of the ingredients for 30 minutes, stirring frequently. Add the fig leaf. Cook for 5-7 more minutes. Remove the leaf, clove, and cinnamon. Put in a cruet to pour over the Buñuelos if desired.

Makes about 20 servings.

Tortitas de Elote (Corn Fritters)

3 cups of fresh corn, cut from the cob, or two cans (15¼-ounce) of whole corn
1¼ cup of honey
½ cup of white flour
pinch of salt
1 cup of vegetable oil, for frying

In a blender or food processor, finely grind the corn. Mix in the honey, flour, pinch of salt, and blend well. Shape into small patties. In a medium skillet, heat the oil until hot, and fry the patties until golden brown. Remove and place them on a serving dish; pour the same syrup as for the Buñuelos over them and serve hot.

Makes about 12-14 pieces.

Flan de Vainilla Expreso (Fast Vanilla Flan)

Flan is not originally a Nicaraguan dish but has become popular over the years in a wide variety of flavors and styles.

4 eggs
1 can of evaporated milk
1 can of sweetened condensed milk
1 pinch of cinnamon
1 cup of milk
4 tablespoons of sugar
1 teaspoon of vanilla extract
1 pinch of salt
2 tablespoons of water
½ cup of water, for steaming

In a medium bowl, combine the condensed, evaporated, and regular milks until well blended. Add the vanilla, salt, cinnamon, and eggs. Mix well. In a 5- to 6-cup aluminum or stainless steel bowl, dissolve the sugar in 2 tablespoons of water. Over low heat and with oven mitts on, so you don't get burned, turn the bowl slowly over the flame while angling it to the sides to melt and caramelize the sugar. When the sugar is caramelized, set aside to cool. Slowly add the egg-milk mixture to the bowl; cover it with aluminum foil.

Place the bowl over a double boiler with water in the bottom section for steaming. Cook over medium heat for 1 hour. Turn to low if boiling too hard. Remove pan from heat and let sit until cool; remove and refrigerate. (If using a pressure cooker, cook for 25 minutes; if using a conventional oven, cook for 1½ hours).

With a flexible spatula, carefully separate the edges of the flan from the bowl. Turn the bowl upside down over a serving plate, and give it a sudden downwards shake to make it disengage.

Serves 6-8.

Flan de Vainilla (Crème Brulée)

1 cup of half-and-half milk
1 teaspoon of vanilla extract
5 egg yolks
½ cup of sugar

Heat oven to 325°F. In a saucepan, combine the half-and-half with the vanilla; cook over low heat until just hot, then turn off heat, and let sit for a few minutes.

In a bowl, beat the egg yolks and sugar together. Stir in about a half of the milk mixture. Pour into a large ovenproof ramekin (or 4 individual-sized ones, if you prefer). Cover tightly with aluminum foil. Place ramekin in a larger baking dish; fill dish halfway with boiling water. Bake for about 30 minutes, until the center is barely set. Cool. Refrigerate for 2-3 days.

When ready to serve, allow to stand in kitchen to reach room temperature. Top the custard with a thin layer of sugar (about 4 teaspoons). Place the ramekin in a broiler 2-3 inches from heat source. Turn on broiler. Cook until sugar melts and browns, or for 4-5 minutes; watch carefully, so it doesn't turn black. Serve while still warm.

Serves 4.

Flan de Chocolate (Chocolate Flan)

½ cup of sugar
2 tablespoons of water
1 can (8-ounces) of sweetened condensed milk
4 eggs
1 can (12 ounces) of evaporated milk
pinch of salt
1 cup of milk
3 squares (2 ounces each) of semisweet baking chocolate
½ cup of water, for steaming

In a 5- to 6-cup aluminum or stainless steel bowl, dissolve the sugar in 2 tablespoons of water. Over low heat, and wearing mittens on so you don't get burned, turn the bowl slowly over the flame, angling it to the side to thoroughly melt and caramelize the sugar. When caramelized, set aside to cool.

Mix the 3 milks, vanilla, sugar, and salt, in a large bowl, with an electric mixer or whisk. Melt the chocolate in a double boiler. When melted, slowly pour the chocolate in with the milks; mix thoroughly. Add the eggs, and beat for another minute. Pour into the bowl containing the caramelized sugar. Cover tightly with aluminum foil.

Place the bowl in a double boiler with the water for steaming in the bottom section. Cook over medium heat for 1 hour. If boiling too hard, turn to low. Turn the burner off and let sit until cool; remove and refrigerate.

Carefully, separate the flan from the sides of the bowl using a flexible spatula. Turn the bowl upside down over a serving plate; disengage the flan with a sudden downwards motion.

Serves 6-8.

Flan Clásico (Classic Flan)

1 cup plus 4 tablespoons of sugar
2 tablespoons of water
3 eggs, deveined
3 egg yolks
2 cups of milk
1 teaspoon of vanilla extract
1 cinnamon stick, 2-inch long
pinch of salt
2-inch strip lime rind
½ cup of water, for steaming

Preheat oven to 375°F.

Dissolve 4 tablespoons of sugar in 2 tablespoons of water, using an aluminum or stainless steel bowl, and caramelize the mixture over the open flame of a burner set to low heat. Be sure to use oven mitts, when holding the bowl, so as not to burn your fingers. With a wire whisk, lightly beat the eggs and egg yolks together. Add the milk, remaining sugar, salt, vanilla, cinnamon stick, and lime rind. Whisk until well blended. Pour the mixture into the caramelized bowl. Cover it with aluminum foil.

Put the foil covered in a large pan, holding ½ cup of water, for steaming. (The water should come halfway up the sides of the bowl.) Put in the oven and bake for about one hour or until an inserted toothpick comes out clean. Take out of the oven to cool, but still leave in the water to finish setting. When cool, remove from the water and put in the refrigerator.

When ready to serve and with a flexible spatula, carefully free the flan all around the edges of the bowl and invert the bowl over a serving dish. Dislodge the flan onto the dish with a sudden, sharp, downwards motion. Cut in wedges with a cake knife and serve.

Serves about 6-8.

Budin de Pan (Bread Pudding)

8 cups of old bread, cut up
½ gallon of milk, more if needed
2 cups of sugar
3 eggs
12 prunes, quartered
¼ teaspoon of nutmeg
½ teaspoon of powdered cinnamon
1 teaspoon of vanilla extract
pinch of salt
2 tablespoons of dark rum (optional)

Preheat oven to 400°F. In a large bowl, put the bread and enough milk to cover. Let soak until soft. As the bread expands, add more milk to keep it covered. When bread is totally soft, beat it with an electric mixer. Add the sugar, salt, cinnamon, nutmeg, vanilla, and prunes. Mix well. Blend the eggs and add to the bread mixture. Beat until everything is thoroughly mixed in.

Pour the mixture into a greased, lightly floured pan (9 x 12 x 3 inches) and place in the heated oven for about 1 hour. It's done when an inserted toothpick comes out clean. Sprinkle powdered sugar on top.

Serves 12-14.

Viejitas (Little Sweet Tortes)

½ pound of white corn
½ pound of *sincho* cheese
¼ pound of ground *piloncillo* or brown sugar
¼ cup of shortening
1 cup of water

Cook the white corn in the water until soft. Discard the water, rinse the corn, and then grind it together with the cheese. Add the shortening and mix well.

Make little oval dumplings about 1½-inch wide. Put ½ teaspoon of ground piloncillo or brown sugar on top of each. On a greased cookie sheet, bake for about 12-15 minutes, in a preheated oven at 350°F, until golden.

Makes about 50 pieces.

Tres Leches (Three Milks)

For Cake

6 eggs
½ cup of milk
2 cups of all purpose white flour
1½ teaspoons of baking powder
2 cups of sugar
3 tablespoons of vanilla extract
pinch of salt

Preheat the oven to 400°F. Thoroughly mix all of the above ingredients. Pour into a greased, lightly floured cake pan about 8 x 11 x 2 inches. Bake in a preheated oven at 375°F for about 20 minutes. Test it with a toothpick inserted in the middle; when it comes out clean, remove from the oven and set aside. Leave the oven on.

For Syrup

4 eggs, separated
1½ cups of sugar
2 cans of sweetened condensed milk
1 can of evaporated milk
1 lemon peel

1½ cups of corn syrup
½ cup of cherry juice
½ cup of milk

While the cake is baking, blend the 4 egg yolks, 1 cup of sugar, ½ cup of milk, 2 cans of sweetened condensed milks, and 1 can of evaporated milk. Beat the 4 egg whites, until they rise; add ½ cup sugar and continue beating, until they form stiff peaks. Heat the corn syrup and the lemon peel in a saucepan, and stir for a minute. Remove from burner; slowly add the cherry juice and the beaten egg whites.

Poke small holes on the cake and pour in the 3 milks mixture. Lift the sides and pour some more underneath, making sure the whole cake is saturated with it. Finally, pour the corn syrup mixture over the cake, return to the oven and cook for another 12-15 minutes at 375°F. Remove and let cool.

Serves 8-10.

Dulce de Batata/Boniato
(Sweet Potato and Almond Custard)

This is a favorite dessert of my family and friends. Also known as Que Bien me Sabe.

1 quart of milk
5 teaspoons of rice
2½ tablespoons of cornstarch
2 cups of sugar
1 medium *batata/boniato* (sweet potato), peeled, grated
1½-ounce of blanched-slivered almonds (Hard to find sometimes but can substitute with ground almonds; they are found in baked-goods area)
pinch of salt

Soak the rice in ½ cup of warm milk and set aside. Meanwhile, peel the sweet potato and grate it.

Dissolve the cornstarch in ¼ cup of milk. In a medium saucepan over low-medium heat, put the remaining milk and the soaked rice in milk. Cook until rice is very soft. Slowly add the cornstarch mixture, sugar, and salt, stirring continuously. Add the sweet potato and almonds. Simmer, stirring constantly, until mixture develops a thick, pudding-like consistency. Place in a ceramic bowl or large ramekin, and refrigerate overnight.

Serves 8.

Natilla de Arroz (Rice Pudding)

1 cup of sugar
½ teaspoon of salt
1 cup of cooked rice
2 teaspoons of vanilla extract
4 whole eggs, beaten in a large bowl
1 quart of milk
nutmeg powder, to sprinkle
¼ teaspoon of cinnamon powder
2 cinnamon sticks, 2-inch long

Mix the sugar, salt, rice, cinnamon powder, and vanilla with the beaten eggs. In a medium saucepan, bring milk just to boiling; add the rice mixture and the cinnamon sticks. Cook over low heat, stirring constantly, for about 40 minutes. Set aside and sprinkle with the nutmeg. Serve warm or at room temperature. In this version, the rice is like a custard.

Variation: Preheat oven to 375°F. Mix the sugar, salt, rice, cinnamon powder, and vanilla with the beaten eggs. Bring milk just to boiling, add the rice mixture, and cinnamon sticks; mix well. Pour into buttered, 2-quart casserole dish, and set dish into a pan with enough water for steaming. Bake for 1 hour. It is done when inserted knife comes out clean. Sprinkle top of pudding with nutmeg. In this version, the rice is dryer.

Arroz con Leche (Rice Pudding)

½ pound of rice
2 cups of water
2 cinnamon sticks, 2-inch long
2 cups of sugar
pinch of salt
2 cups of milk
2 teaspoons of vanilla extract
nutmeg powder, to sprinkle

Wash the rice thoroughly. In a medium saucepan, add the water, rice, cinnamon sticks, and salt. Cook at low heat, until the water has evaporated; add the milk, vanilla, and sugar. Continue cooking, until the rice has burst open and has a fluffy consistency, with some liquid remaining. Remove. Set aside to cool.

I have used condensed milk instead of regular milk to make a richer pudding; in this case, only 1 cup of sugar is required.

Pastel de Pio V (Pope Pius V Cake)

Syrup

4 cups of sugar
4 cups of water
1 cinnamon stick, 2-inch long
10 cloves, whole
lime peel
½ cup of dark rum
1 cup of raisins

This is one of our most traditional and delicious desserts. Although it is somewhat tedious to prepare—since it consists of 4 parts: syrup, cake, custard, and meringue—I am sure the end result will please you.

Put the sugar, water, cinnamon stick, cloves, and lime peel in a saucepan. Bring to a boil over medium heat, until it has a light, syrupy consistency. Remove from heat and let cool. Strain. Add the dark rum and raisins; mix with a spoon and set aside.

Marquesote (Cake)

8 egg whites
3 teaspoons of baking powder
6 ounces of *pinol* (very fine white corn meal)
1 teaspoon of baking soda
4 ounces of all-purpose white flour
6 ounces of sugar

Preheat oven at 350°F. Grease a rectangular (8 x 11 x 2 inches) baking pan; cover it inside with wax paper all around. Beat the egg whites in a separate bowl, until they have the consistency of mayonnaise. Gradually add the sugar while continuing to beat—stop when thoroughly mixed in. Combine the corn meal and flour with the baking soda; slowly blend in the egg-white-sugar mixture, continuing to beat until all ingredients are well mixed and there are no lumps. Add the baking powder, beat well, and pour the mixture into the baking pan.

Use a spatula to even out the surface of the batter, and place the pan in the oven. Bake for 15-20 minutes or until lightly browned (when a toothpick inserted in the center of the cake comes out clean, it's done). Let the cake cool. Carefully, remove it from the pan and peel off the wax paper. Return the cake to the baking pan and pour the syrup over it, making sure to soak it completely.

Custard

4 egg yolks
1 can (4-ounces) of sweetened condensed milk
2 cups of whole milk
2 teaspoons of vanilla extract
1 tablespoon of cornstarch
1 tablespoon of butter

In a blender, mix thoroughly the sweetened condensed milk, whole milk, vanilla, cornstarch, and butter. Add the egg yolks and blend in thoroughly. Place the ingredients in a saucepan over medium heat and stir constantly until thick. If you prefer a thicker custard, add a little more cornstarch. Stir until the custard reaches the desired consistency. Remove from heat and let cool. Pour the custard over the cake and spread evenly.

Meringue

3 egg whites
²/₃ cup of sugar
¼ teaspoon of cream of tartar
½ cup of dry prunes, cut into pieces

Beat the egg whites, sugar, and cream of tartar together until well mixed and fluffy. Spread over the custard. Garnish with cut-up, dried prunes and serve.

Serves 12-16.

Maduros en Gloria (Plantain Flambé)

6 very ripe yellow plantains (or large ripe bananas), peeled, sliced
    lengthwise
½ cup of brown sugar
6 tablespoons of butter

½ cup of light cream
¼ cup of sour cream
¼ cup of *sincho* cheese
dash of cinnamon
2 tablespoons of dark rum

Heat the oven at 350°F. Fry the plantains in 5 tablespoons of butter over medium heat until light golden. Grease a rectangular oven dish with remaining butter, and arrange the plantains in the dish. Mix the cheese with the sugar and dash of cinnamon. Spread the cheese mixture over the plantains. Blend the cream, sour cream, and dark rum together; pour over the plantains. Bake in middle rack of the oven, for about 35-40 minutes.

Serves 10-12.

DRINKS

Atole de Maiz (Hot Corn Drink)

2 tablespoons of cornstarch
5 cups of milk (or water)
1 cinnamon stick, 2-inch long
1 teaspoon of vanilla extract
5 tablespoons of sugar, or to taste
dash of salt
cinnamon powder for sprinkling
two 8-ounce cans of sweet whole corn

Put the corn with its water in a blender and process it until
well mashed. Drain and force through a sieve; reserve. Discard
the corn skins. Dissolve the cornstarch in 1 cup of milk. In
medium saucepan, bring the milk, vanilla, sugar, salt, and
cinnamon stick to a boil. Slowly add the dissolved cornstarch
and the sieved corn to the milk. Turn heat to low. Cook,
stirring, until mixture is somewhat thickened, for about 12-
16 minutes. Serve immediately in large mugs. Can be served
cold in summer.

Serves 3-4.

Atole de Plátano (Hot Plantain Drink)

2 tablespoons of cornstarch
5 tablespoons of sugar, or to taste

4 cups of water
1 cinnamon stick, 2-inch long
dash of salt
1 large green plantain

Peel the plantain and boil in a cup of water until soft. Remove from water and let it cool; reserve the water. Cut lengthwise and remove inside vein. In a blender, put the plantain, the boiled water, plus a cup of water; process until well mixed. Add the cornstarch, sugar, and salt; blend until soupy.

In a medium saucepan, heat the rest of the water with the cinnamon stick. Slowly add the plantain mixture to the water while stirring; bring to a boil over medium-low heat. Cook for 12-15 minutes, till mixture has thickened. Serve immediately in large mugs.

Serves 4-5.

Chicha de Piña con Gengibre (Pineapple-Ginger Drink)

1 very ripe pineapple
3 cups of sugar
6 cups of water
4 cloves
1 quart of orange juice
2 cinnamon sticks, 2-inch long
4 pieces of ginger root, 2½- to 3-inch long

This drink is also called Chicha de Coyolitos; unfortunately the coyolito fruits (which are small sweet fruits berry like), are not available in the States. However, this drink tastes almost like the real thing back home.

Trim the ends of the pineapple. Remove the skin and cut out the indentations. Save the fruit for eating or making juice later on. Peel the ginger and cut it in chunks.

Cut the pineapple skin in small pieces and place in a food processor or blender with the ginger pieces and two cups of water. Blend the mixture thoroughly; force through a sieve and discard the pulp. Add the sugar, water, and rest of ingredients. Cover and let ferment at room temperature for a couple of days. When ready to serve, remove the cinnamon sticks and cloves; serve over crushed ice with a slice of pineapple. It should taste somewhat alcoholic.

Makes about 8-10 glasses.

Fresco de Piña y Arroz (Pineapple-and-Rice Drink)

1 very ripe pineapple
½ cup of white rice, uncooked
2 cups of sugar, or to taste
8 cups of water

Trim the ends of the pineapple. Remove the skin and cut out the indentations. Save the fruit for eating or making juice later on. Place the skin in a large stockpot with enough water to cover by about 1 inch. Bring to a boil and cook, uncovered, for about 10 minutes.

Add the rice. Keep boiling until the rice begins to fluff. Remove from the heat and let cool. Strain first through a colander, then force through a sieve, discarding the mash. Measure the amount of strained liquid and add an equal amount of water. Add the sugar and stir until dissolved. Serve over ice.

Serves 8-10.

Refresco de Piña (Pineapple Drink)

1 ripe pineapple
6 cups of water
2 cups of sugar
pinch of salt
crushed ice

Fresh fruit juices are so essential to the way of life in Nicaragua that they are served every midmorning as a fortifier and a thirst quencher. You will find them served at any time in the restaurants.

Remove the pineapple skin and cut out the indentations; use it for one of the recipes above. Cut the pineapple meat in chunks and put in the blender with the water, salt, and sugar. Put it in a large pitcher. Check for sweetness and add sugar as needed. Serve immediately over crushed ice. (If serving later, refrigerate without ice until ready to serve.)

Serves 6.

Refresco de Naranja or Naranjada (Orangeade)

6 juice oranges
1 cup of sugar
6 cups of water
pinch of salt
crushed ice

Squeeze the oranges; add the water, pinch of salt, and the sugar, to taste.

When ready to serve, pour over the crushed ice.

We make refreshments out of any fruit or combination of fruits. If you want pure juice, don't add any water, but remember that orangeade is more refreshing than pure juice in very hot weather.

Serves 6.

Chicha de Maiz (Fermented Corn Drink)

3 pounds of dry white corn
½ pound of sugar
1 sugarcane, 10- to 15-inch long, peeled, sliced
2 tablespoons of vanilla extract
2 gallons of water
3-5 drops of red food dye

Wash the corn and let it soak in a large bowl with enough water to cover, until it gets tender. Remove any floating skins; rinse and drain the corn. Put in a large pot with 1 gallon of water. Bring to a boil. Remove from burner. Set aside in a covered large ceramic bowl.

Next day, add the peeled sugarcane in slices to accelerate the fermentation. Add the sugar in equal parts each day for the next 5 days. On the sixth day, add the dye. Mix. Add the rest of the water, vanilla, and sugar to taste. Serve over ice.

Makes 25-30 glasses.

Horchata (Almond-Rice Drink)

¼ pound of almond, finely ground
½ cup of white rice
1 teaspoon of vanilla extract
2 cinnamon sticks, 2-inch long
4 cups of milk
⅛ teaspoon of allspice
2 cups of water
1 tablespoon of shredded coconut

In a medium bowl, soak the rice for 2 hours in the 2 cups of water. Meanwhile, grind the almonds in a blender or food processor (or buy them already ground). Finely grind the rice; add the ground almonds and remaining ingredients and blend thoroughly. Serve immediately over crushed ice in a tall glass, or refrigerate to serve later over ice.

Serves 8.

Agua de Arroz (Rice Water Drink)

½ pound of white rice
6 cups of water
juice of 3 limes (substitute with 1 cup of pineapple juice, or 1
    cup of orange juice)
1½ cups of sugar
2 cinnamon sticks, 2-inch long
1 teaspoon of vanilla extract
pinch of salt

In a medium saucepan, cook the rice and cinnamon sticks in 3 cups of water over medium-low heat, until the rice bursts open. Remove from heat and let cool. Add the lime, or other juice, and the remaining ingredients. Check for sweetness. Serve over crushed ice. When forced through a sieve, this drink is also served to infants as a fortifier.

Serves 6.

Pinolillo (Cocoa Drink with Corn)

1 pound of dried white corn, roasted
½ pound of cocoa beans, roasted
1 tablespoon of cinnamon powder
½ tablespoon of allspice powder
3 quarts of water
1 cup of sugar, or to taste

This drink can be cooked at a slow boil for about 12-15 minutes, until it thickens. In Nicaragua, we call it chocolate, because the cocoa beans add the flavor of chocolate.

The whole dried white corn and cocoa beans are found at the Mexican markets, unroasted. To roast, put them in an iron skillet over medium heat. Stir frequently, so as not to burn them. Cook them for about 20-30 minutes. Grind together into a fine powder. (Sometimes the roasted cocoa beans and white corn can also be found already ground in the Mexican stores.)

Combine the powdered corn-and-cocoa-bean mixture with the allspice and cinnamon. This mixture can be kept up to a year. The amounts given above make a large supply; you might want to reduce the amounts to suit your needs. To make an individual serving, put 2 tablespoons of powder in 1 cup of water, and add 3 tablespoons of sugar, to taste. Can be boiled and served hot or just stirred and served cold—add crushed ice if serving cold.

Makes approximately 20 glasses.

Tiste (Corn Drink with Cocoa)

2 pounds of tortillas
½ pound of roasted cocoa beans, finely ground
2 tablespoons of cinnamon powder
1½ tablespoons of allspice powder
3 quarts of water
1 cup of sugar, or to taste

Soak the tortillas for about 2 hours, in enough water to soften them. Place in a blender, add 1 quart of water, and process to a paste. Add the rest of the water and the remaining ingredients, and blend thoroughly. Check for sweetness. Add crushed ice and serve immediately.

The tortilla paste, mixed with the ground cocoa beans, cinnamon, and allspice, will keep in the refrigerator for up to a week, wrapped in aluminum foil. When ready to serve, add water to desired thickness and pour over crushed ice.

Serves about 20 glasses.

Cereal (Corn-Cereal Drink)

1 pound of dried white corn, roasted, ground
3 ounces of ground almond
3 ounces of fast-cooking oatmeal, ground
3 ounces of ground sorghum, white or yellow
3 ounces of white rice, finely ground
2 tablespoons of cinnamon powder
1½ tablespoons of allspice powder
1 cup of sugar, or to taste
½ gallon of water (or milk)

Roast the grains and then grind them together into a fine powder. Dissolve the sugar in the water or milk. Add the powder and remaining ingredients. Blend until smooth. Serve over ice.

(The dry mixture can be kept tightly closed for months.)

Serves 10-12.

Tibio (White-Corn Drink)

½ pound of roasted dried white corn, finely ground
½ gallon of water
sugar to taste (optional)

Mix together; bring to a slow boil for about 12 minutes, until it thickens. Serve warm.

Serves about 10.

Café con Leche (Milk with Coffee)

2 cups of milk
1 teaspoon of sugar
1 teaspoon of instant coffee

Those of us growing up in Nicaragua found this drink—especially for breakfast—to be essential to life!

In a small saucepan under moderate to low heat, bring the milk to a slow boil. Add the coffee and sugar, and stir. Remove from the burner and serve in a coffee mug. If using a microwave, mix the ingredients in a mug and microwave about 2 minutes or until hot.

Serves 2.

GLOSSARY

achiote paste. Annatto seed mashed into a paste with onions, garlic, cumin, oregano, and lime juice or vinegar. Now available in many Mexican markets and supermarket's specialty sections.

Antojitos, Bocas, Boquitas. Little tapas of appetizers or beans, grilled meat, sausage, etc., served with cocktails.

Arroz. White long-grained rice is preferred. We stir-fry it lightly in oil before cooking to make it fluffy and flavorful.

Atole. A gritty, thick cornmeal drink that can be drunk hot or cold.

Atolillo. A thick Atole-like custard that is served as a dessert rather than a drink.

banana leaves. Actually refers to plantain leaves. Used for wrapping tamales, for cooking, and for serving.

Batata/Boniato. Resembles a sweet potato but with a white instead of orange flesh, and no sweetness. Should be hard when purchased and used.

Budin. Just like the common American bread pudding but with prunes, or raisins, and cinnamon sticks.

Buñuelos. Fried dumplings or patties of yucca dough served with cinnamon and sugar.

cacao. Cocoa beans

Carne Asada. Charcoal-grilled beef

chayote. Pretty pale green crispy squash, shaped like a pear. It should be peeled and the seed be removed before cooking.

chicha. Drink made of dried fermented corn with sugarcane and sugar. Slightly alcoholic.

chicharron. Fried pork rind or crackling, cooked until crunchy and the fat is rendered out. Lard comes from this fat. It is served hot or cold in appetizers or as a main dish.

congo peppers. Small dark green chili, shaped like a raindrop. Very spicy. So far, I have only found them in Miami and Los Angeles. Can substitute for serrano or jalapeño pepper.

chorizo. Spicy pork sausage with a strong annatto flavor and red in color. It comes in mild, medium, and hot spicy flavors.

cilantro. Known as coriander or Chinese parsley. It is used, fresh and dried, as a seasoning.

comal. Deep dish made of lava rock or hard mud in which to make tortillas and toast cocoa or coffee beans

culantro. Its thin, elongated, serrated leaf and its pungent, unique aroma give this herb its characteristic flavor. It's often mistaken for cilantro, although it doesn't look or taste anything like it. It is commonly used in Nicaragua. It is widely grown in Miami, and I have recently begun to see it in the Mexican markets in Chicago.

Enchiladas. Fried tortillas filled with meat, cheese, or beans, and sauce on top. This is different from the Mexican Enchilada dish.

flan. Custard-like dessert

Frijoles. Beans. Black beans are most common in Cuba; red and white beans, in Nicaragua; pinto beans, in Mexico. They are served any time of the day.

Gazpacho. A cold tomato soup containing a variety of raw vegetables and no meat

Horchata. Almond-and-rice drink mashed together

kiosko. Kiosk. Little roofed buildings or stands, generally in or near a park, with tables and chairs nearby, where snacks and drinks are served.

malanga. Taro root. Known as quequisque in Nicaragua. Taro is a tuberous root vegetable, shaped like a yam. It has a thin brown skin and white—to cream-colored flesh. Like cassava root (yucca), you may be able to find it bagged in the frozen section.

masa harina. Corn flour used to make tortillas and tamales

merienda. Snack

Mexican squash. Pale green squash with white speckles. Tastes like zucchini.

Mondongo. Known as menudo or tripe. Literally, the lining of the stomach.

Naranja Agria. Sour oranges or bitter oranges. In Florida, they go under the name of Seville oranges. The juice is used as a marinade for all kinds of meats. I just started seeing them fresh in Chicago, and sometimes, I have seen the juice bottled at the supermarkets. However, you can make a close approximation by combining the juice of one lime with the juice of one grapefruit.

piloncillo. Unrefined cane sugar. It is brown and comes in very hard cone-shaped pieces that must be ground up before using.

plantains. They look like large bananas, but they have a slightly different flavor. Unripe plantains are green and firm. Ripe plantains are yellow, orange, brown, or black in color, in increasing order of ripeness. When black, they are very ripe, and the inside is syrupy—perfect as a dessert when fried. The darker the skin, the sweeter the taste.

queso añejo. Semidry, crumbly cheese resembling Muenster; Slightly salty. Good for making Revueltas.

queso cotija. Semidry, less crumbly than añejo cheese. I also use it to make Revueltas, if I can't find the añejo or sincho. Nice for stuffing Pescozón with.

queso del Caribe. Soft cheese, excellent for frying or for eating in salads or with beans.

queso fresco. Fresh cheese or farmer's cheese. It has a lightly salty taste and smooth texture, reminiscent of cream cheese.

queso sincho. Very dry, salty, and crumbly cheese. It is my favorite to use when making Revueltas.

tortillas. A flat round pancake of various sizes and thickness made out of masa harina. Very popular in Mexico and Central America. (In Spain, tortillas are actually egg omelets.)

turtle eggs. Huevos de Paslama are eaten boiled with salt, chili, and lime juice.

yucca. Cassava or manioc root. It is covered by a tough brown skin almost like a bark; the inside is a hard white flesh with a woody vein in the middle, which should be removed. Some stores have it in the frozen section already peeled, cut, and bagged.

Tips

Beans—Always check the beans as I often have found pebbles. Soak beans in warm water for at least 3 hours, before cooking, to remove impurities. Or, place the beans in a pan with enough water to cover them, and boil them hard for 2-3 minutes. Discard the water. Rinse. Cook per instructions. I have learned that adding a piece of peeled ginger helps in the digestion of the beans.

Bell Peppers—Green, red, or yellow bell peppers are always fried first as they take a little longer to soften.

Chayote—Chayote squash is used many times in place of potatoes. It adds a subtle flavor to the food. Yucca and plantain are also used as substitutes.

Chicken—We wash and rinse the chicken thoroughly in cold water then rub lime juice all over it—inside the cavity, too. We also put salt and garlic inside the cavity before cooking.

Cilantro—Chopped cilantro is used throughout our cooking. Add to scrambled eggs before serving to provide a unique flavor.

Dried Corn Husk—Used to wrap tamales. Soak them in hot boiled water for 10 minutes. Remove. Separate. Drain. Soaking makes them pliable and easy to fold.

Flans—They taste best when made 1 day before serving.

Gallo Pinto—Can be kept frozen for up to a year. When ready to eat, thaw it out. In a large skillet, add 1 tablespoon of olive oil, fry some onions until translucent, add 2 cups of gallo pinto, and fry for about 10-12 minutes, turning frequently with a spatula, until the rice gets crispy.

Mint—Used throughout our cooking, especially in soups.

Legumes—When cooking any type of legumes (peas, beans, and lentils), be sure to always spread them first over the counter and remove the little stones that so frequently find their way into the package.

Plantain—To peel plantains, first cut them in half. Make a shallow lengthwise cut over the skin, enough to get to the meat. Under running cold water, pry open the sides of the cut skin with a knife until the skin comes off. If the plantain is green and fresh, the skin will come off easily; otherwise, you might have to pry it several times. Follow this same procedure when peeling yucca.

Queso Frito—Queso del Caribe is delicious when fried and eaten with hot corn tortillas or Tostones.

Revueltas—Don't throw away old Revueltas; they can be reheated the next day on a comal or flat skillet, or even in the toaster, and they taste delicious.

Rice—If cooking with long-grained rice, the cooking time increases to 50 minutes rather than 25 minutes as for Arborio rice. Back home, we would rinse the rice, drain it, and let it dry before cooking it. This is no longer necessary, and probably, this loses vitamins. Never throw out leftover rice as you can use it in several of the recipes listed here.

Serrano Chili Peppers—Use them in place of congo peppers, which are found only in Miami or Los Angeles.

Soups/Stews—Our soups and stews taste best if cooked the day before serving; they gather the flavors better.

Sour Cream—I often use yogurt as a substitute, as it is healthier and less fattening.

Tortilla—To warm tortillas in the microwave, wrap them in a wet paper towel, put them inside a plastic bag, and place the bag in the middle of the microwave. Use 10 seconds per tortilla.

To heat them in an oiled skillet on medium heat, lightly sprinkle the tortilla with water before adding to the skillet.

Heat each side for 15 seconds. Serve wrapped in a cloth napkin.

When making your own tortillas, to be sure that they are cooking on the inside, press and pat the tortilla down, all around, with a folded paper towel after flipping it to the other side. The top layer should rise up, creating a pocket, much like pita bread. You especially want the pocket when stuffing them as in making Enchiladas.

Don't throw away old tortillas; they can be use in other dishes listed here.

Index

Lightning Source UK Ltd.
Milton Keynes UK
10 January 2011
165435UK00001B/331/A